IMAGES
of America

CARONDELET

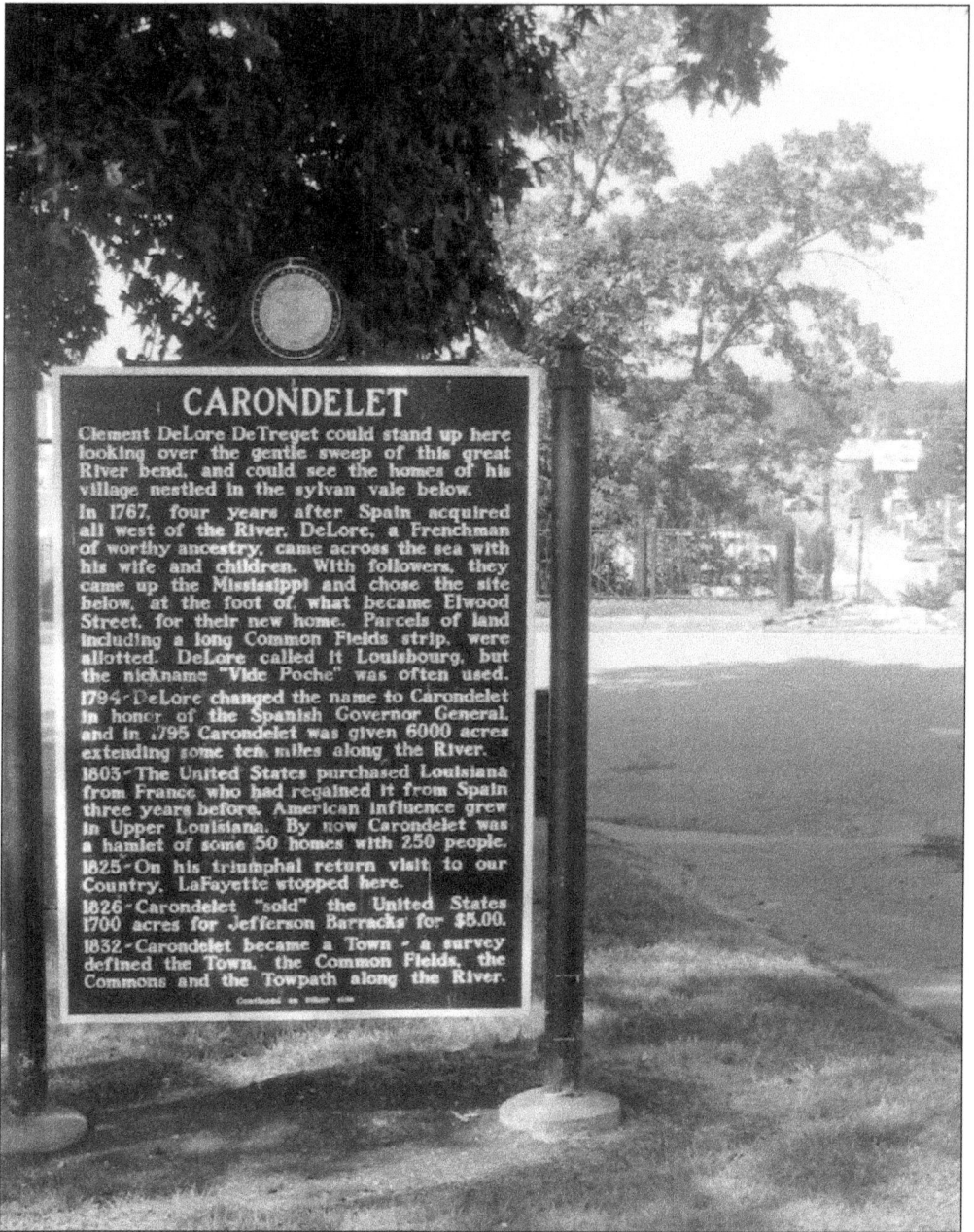

This marker in Bellerive Park placed by the Carondelet Historical Society overlooks the site where Clement DeLor de Treget founded the village of Carondelet in 1767. Bellerive Park offers a wonderful view onto South Broadway and the Mississippi River. (Photograph by John A. Wright Sr.)

On the cover: Please see page 80. (Courtesy of the Carondelet Historical Society.)

IMAGES
of America

CARONDELET

John A. Wright Sr. and Sylvia A. Wright

ARCADIA
PUBLISHING

Published by Arcadia Publishing
Charleston, South Carolina

Library of Congress Catalog Card Number: 2007940137

For all general information contact Arcadia Publishing at:
Telephone 843-853-2070
Fax 843-853-0044
E-mail sales@arcadiapublishing.com
For customer service and orders:
Toll-Free 1-888-313-2665

Visit us on the Internet at www.arcadiapublishing.com

*To all those who have worked to preserve the history of
Carondelet for present and future generations*

CONTENTS

ACKNOWLEDGMENTS

A very special thanks goes to the South Broadway Merchants Association and president Jaymes Dearing for requesting that we write this book. It has truly been a delightful and rewarding experience for us. A deep word of gratitude also goes to Ron Bolte, president of the Carondelet Historical Society, and his assistants Mary Ann Simon and Lois Waningor along with the host of volunteers who through the years have collected, organized, and preserved thousands of documents on the history of the community. There is no question that this project could not have occurred without the unending assistance of the Carondelet Historical Society, a true community treasure. A special thanks also goes to the Carondelet branch of the St. Louis Public Library for providing invaluable assistance and information.

Acknowledgment must be given to three special individuals who paved the way for this book through their earlier research, writing, and enthusiasm for the history of Carondelet. Specifically we wish to thank Nini Harris, author of *History of Carondelet*, published in 1991; Carolyn Hewes Toft, author of *Carondelet—The Ethnic Heritage of an Urban Neighborhood*; and Norbury L. Wayman, author of *The History of St. Louis Neighborhoods—Carondelet*, published in 1978.

Thanks also goes to special individuals and institutions for their help and support in making this book possible. The individuals are Charles Brown; Audrey Newcomer; Verna Murphy; Doris Wesly; Sr. Jane Behlmann, CSJ; Kris Pelizzaro; James Brown; state representative Tom Villa; Marc E. Kollbaum; Janet Wilzbach; Gerald Brooks; and Sharon Doland. The institutions we would like to thank are Mercantile Library, Western Manuscript Collection, University of Missouri–St. Louis; St. Louis Public Library, main branch and Carondelet branch; Carondelet Historical Society; St. Louis Public School Archives; Sisters of St. Joseph of Carondelet Archives; Spanish Society; Archdiocese of St. Louis Archives; Jefferson Barracks Archives; St. Louis Landmarks Association; St. Louis County Parks Department; Midwest Jesuit Archives; Eugene Field House and Toy Museum; City of St. Louis; Sumner High School; and Corinthian Baptist Church.

If anyone's name has been omitted, please accept our apology. You know who you are and what your contribution has added to this publication.

INTRODUCTION

The community of Carondelet, which lies just a few miles south of downtown St. Louis, has a long and rich history that dates back prior to the discovery of America. It was once the home of Native Americans. The last Native American mound, which gave the city of St. Louis its name "Mound City," located at Ohio Avenue and South Broadway, is the only reminder of their earlier presence. The first known Europeans came to the area in 1702 as Catholic missionaries to minister to the Native Americans and built a settlement on an island at the mouth of the River Des Peres. The settlement was short-lived, and the island has even vanished. Only the stream—River of the Fathers—bears witness to its existence. The village that was later named Carondelet was founded in 1767 by Clement DeLor de Treget, who was traveling down the Mississippi River looking for a site to build a home for his family. He chose the foot of what is now Elwood Street, near the river but above the flood stage. He was later joined by other Frenchmen from Cahokia and Kaskaskia. DeLor, vested with possible authority from the Spanish government, assigned town lots to settlers and extensive common fields that were jointly owned and farmed and provided pastureland for the grazing of livestock.

The community's location at the confluence of the Mississippi River and the River Des Peres made it a prime site for the development of industry. The Carondelet Marine Railway on the river proved to be an ideal place for shipbuilding and repair. In 1861, James B. Eads, a successful businessman from St. Louis, used the marine railway to build ironclad gunboats for the Civil War. One of the boats, the *Carondelet*, played a major role in the Battle of Vicksburg.

The Iron Mountain Railroad, which had been completed in 1858, brought iron ore from southern Missouri and linked Carondelet to St. Louis. By the 1870s, Carondelet was home of Jupiter Iron Works, the largest concern in the world producing pig iron to be converted into steel. Other industries and businesses followed, bringing in an influx of laborers to the community from a variety of ethic backgrounds, and with businesses came relief agencies and service industries. Along with the institutions to serve this growing population came America's first kindergarten established by Susan Blow in 1872.

The 20th century brought on a decline in heavy industry and hardship to the community, followed by the opening of Interstate 55, rerouting traffic around Carondelet, taking away many of the customers from shops along South Broadway.

Today through the work of many community agencies, the community is rebounding, and the residents look to the future with great optimism, seeing ongoing preservations, renovations, and new construction taking place. They have a belief that their children and future generations will inherit a great place to call home.

This book documents Carondelet's history through pictures. It is the story of a community's journey from a small village, to a city, to annexation to the City of St. Louis, and through a proud historic past and decline to present-day revitalization. This is a story of a special place where a community's history has been preserved through its religious, educational, and cultural institutions and one of a few places in St. Louis that gives a glimpse of what old St. Louis may have been like. It is also a special place where many of the ethnic groups that make up this great melting pot that is called America can be found living in harmony.

One

THE BEGINNING

The section of St. Louis known as Carondelet was once the home of Native Americans. This prehistoric mound at Ohio Avenue near South Broadway, known as Sugar Loaf, is the last trace of their early presence and is the only extant mound, of many, in St. Louis. In fact, the mounds gave the city its nickname "Mound City." The first recorded Europeans came to the area in 1702 as Catholic missionaries. This settlement was short-lived. In 1767, Clement DeLor de Treget traveled up the Mississippi River from St. Genevieve to lay the foundation for the Carondelet of today. (Photograph by John A. Wright Sr.)

After Carondelet's founder, Clement DeLor de Treget, built his family home at the foot of what is now Elwood Street, near the river above the flood stages, he was soon joined by other French settlers who migrated from Illinois. The drawing above gives a glimpse of how Carondelet appeared in 1826. (Courtesy of the Carondelet Historical Society.)

This old French-style dwelling known as the Constant Didier home was the last standing residence in the drawing at the top of the page. It was torn down in 1908. (Courtesy of the Carondelet Historical Society.)

On July 8, 1826, twelve residents of Carondelet sold 1,700 acres of their common to the United States government for $5. This tract was later developed by the War Department as Jefferson Barracks. The residents felt the encampment would provide a good place for them to sell their goods. Pictured here is an early drawing of the barracks and the surrounding area. (Courtesy of the Carondelet Historical Society.)

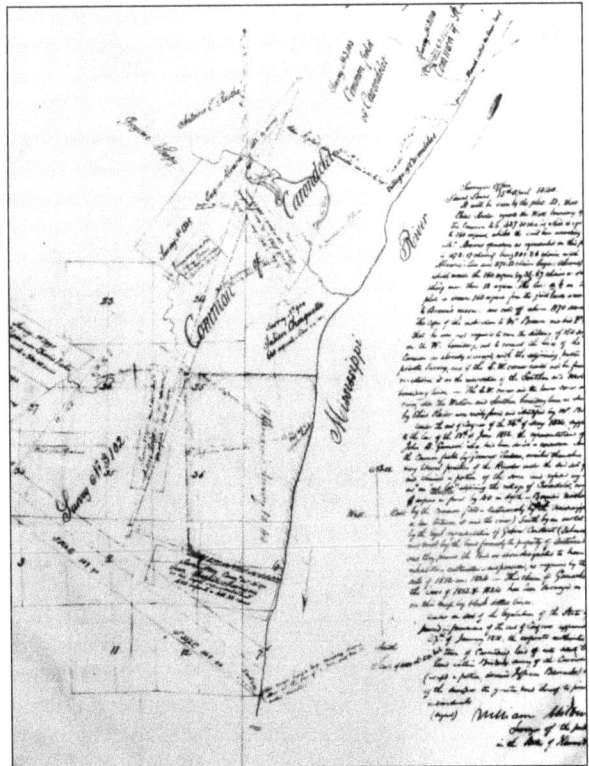

This 1826 survey of the Carondelet community, common, and common fields done by the United States government includes the Jefferson Barracks site. The common fields were divided into strips 1 arpent wide and 40 arpents deep and assigned to individual villagers. The common was used jointly by the villagers for grazing their livestock and also for fuel and wood for building their homes. (Courtesy of the St. Louis County Parks Department.)

Clement DeLor de Treget, Carondelet's founder, first named the settlement Louisborough in honor of Louis XV, then king of France. Neighboring St. Louis residents nicknamed the settlement "Vide Poche," a French term meaning "empty pockets." The settlement was also known by several other names. However, DeLor officially named his village Carondelet in honor of Baron Francois Louis Hector de Carondelet, pictured here in 1794. (Courtesy of the Carondelet Historical Society.)

Pictured here is a copy of the original document signed by Baron Francois Louis Hector de Carondelet, governor general of the Spanish Louisiana Province, which included Carondelet and all the Louisiana Territory. The document was signed on July 7, 1795, in the port of New Orleans establishing the legality of the establishment of the Native American village known as Manchiarnay. (Courtesy of the Mercantile Library.)

On August 27, 1832, with the signatures of two-thirds of the taxable inhabitants on a petition, the county courts (then located in St. Louis city) decreed the incorporation of the town of Carondelet. The town was governed by a five-member board of trustees that occupied the small stone town hall below on Davis Street and the Iron Mountain Railroad tracks. (Courtesy of the Carondelet Historical Society.)

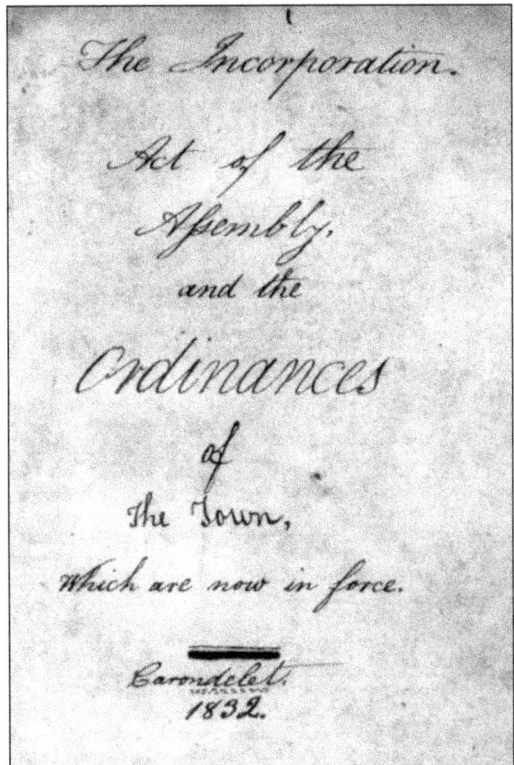

This building served as the town hall as well as the calaboose for those not adhering to the local ordinances. To the south of the hall was a venerable spreading elm tree, under which town meetings were held. (Courtesy of the Carondelet Historical Society.)

The new town trustees immediately began passing ordinances dealing with business regulations, firearms, speeding, peace disturbance, blue laws, working hours of slaves, religious observance, and the chopping of timber. The chopping of fire timber ordinance shown here was important because timber was a major source of income for Carondelet. The fine for breaking this law was $20 for residents and $50 for nonresidents. (Courtesy of the Carondelet Historical Society.)

In 1836, the Sisters of St. Joseph arrived in Carondelet from Lyon, France, at the request of Bishop Joseph Rosati of St. Louis. They moved into this two-room log cabin on the hill next to the Catholic church (now 6400 Minnesota Avenue) and set up one room as a dining room, parlor, and dormitory and the other as a classroom by day and a dormitory by night. (Courtesy of the Sisters of St. Joseph of Carondelet Archives.)

After incorporation, the town continued to grow at a slow but moderate pace. This is an 1841 J. Casper Wild lithograph depicting the view of Carondelet looking down Broadway. Southwardly from Carondelet, the road above was called the road to Herculaneum, and in St. Louis, it was first called the road to Carondelet and later Carondelet Avenue. (Courtesy of the Carondelet Historical Society.)

In 1846, Jacob Stein, a German immigrant glazier, acquired a lot at what is now the southeast corner of Stein and Reilly Streets. He was so impressed by the opportunities in Carondelet that he persuaded many other Germans to come to the village with the assistance of a traveling German society. Because of his efforts, Stein is considered by many to be Carondelet's first immigration agent. (Courtesy of the Carondelet Historical Society.)

Jacob Stein's home, pictured here, is reminiscent of many of the stone homes built by Germans that can still be found in the section of Carondelet that became known as "Stein's Town." Many years later, these German families became prominent in the life of the community. Today the names of Frauss, Schirmer, Nagel, Espenschied, Koeln, and other German names can be found on street signs in this section of Carondelet. (Courtesy of the Carondelet Historical Society.)

Two

FROM VILLAGE TO CITY

The spring of 1849 was the beginning of a new era for Carondelet and a time of great fear. At the dawn of the year, six people contracted cholera in St. Louis. The death toll rose, reaching 86 per day, until fall, when the disease had run its course. The residents of Carondelet began to panic as those fleeing St. Louis looked toward their town for escape. On May 17, 1849, a fire broke out on the steamboat *White Cloud* (above), destroying 23 moored boats and the warehouses along the levee. Carondelet survived unscathed, gaining a reputation for being a healthy and beautiful community. (Courtesy of the Mercantile Library.)

One of the early St. Louis civic leaders to move his family to Carondelet for safety was Judge Wilson Primm. As a lawyer he helped organize the St. Louis Board of Education and in 1843 was elected to the St. Louis Board of Aldermen. Primm was considered a connoisseur and lover of music, and his home became a gathering place for those who loved literature and music. (Courtesy of the Carondelet Historical Society.)

Delphy Carlin, a wealthy trader from New York, arrived in Carondelet in 1848 just prior to the cholera outbreak. He built this fine home known as Delphy Carlin's Villa at the corner of Main Street (now South Broadway) and Davis Street. The home was later purchased in 1882 by John and Maria Krauss for their daughter Julia Rathgeber and her family. Their family continues to occupy the home. (Courtesy of the Carondelet Historical Society.)

Henry Taylor Blow, another well-known St. Louisian who fled the city with his family, acquired 16 acres of land extending west from Virginia and Colorado Avenues and north of Haven Street. He opposed slavery and allied himself with the Free Soil Party and helped fund a group of lawyers who worked on behalf of Dred Scott in his suit for freedom in 1848. He later served as a member of Congress from Missouri and U.S. minister to Brazil and Venezuela. (Courtesy of the Carondelet Historical Society.)

Blow built this mansion at Virginia Avenue, Haven Street, and Loughborough Avenue, which entertained many important and powerful personalities such as Pres. Ulysses S. Grant in 1876. The home was later used by the Missouri Pacific Railroad as its hospital. Before the home was torn down, the library was disassembled and taken to the Missouri Historical Society. (Courtesy of the Carondelet Historical Society.)

Alexander Lyle, Henry Taylor Blow's business partner, joined Blow in Carondelet and built this very fine home during the 1840s and abruptly left the community at the start of the Civil War. Today the home is part of Carondelet Park and is still in use. (Courtesy of the Carondelet Historical Society.)

This is an early picture of the Carondelet Park lake. The 180-acre park was dedicated on July 4, 1876, and added to the St. Louis Park Program. Since it was dedicated on the 100th anniversary of the Declaration of Independence, some thought it should have been named Independence Park. The park was the result of a compromise when citizens in the southern part of St. Louis could not see the value of Forest Park, which was being promoted to them. (Courtesy of Carondelet Historical Society.)

Louis G. Picot, a St. Louis land claims attorney, moved to Carondelet around the same time as Lyle and Blow and built this imitation medieval castle on the 55-foot-tall hill just southeast of St. Joseph Convent at a reported cost of $40,000. The castle tower became a landmark for steamboat captains on the river. When the Civil War was heating up, Picot first flew the Union flag over the castle and within a few days hoisted the Confederate flag and fled the village. (Courtesy of the Carondelet Historical Society.)

This picture offers a glimpse of the village of Carondelet in the mid-1840s. Even with the new arrivals, the village remained mostly rural. Its population grew rather slowly compared to its neighbor St. Louis. In 1799, the settlement had a population of 184, and four years later in 1803, the population had only reached 250 with 50 homes. By 1850, the population reached 1,265, which included 28 enslaved individuals. (Courtesy of the Carondelet Historical Society.)

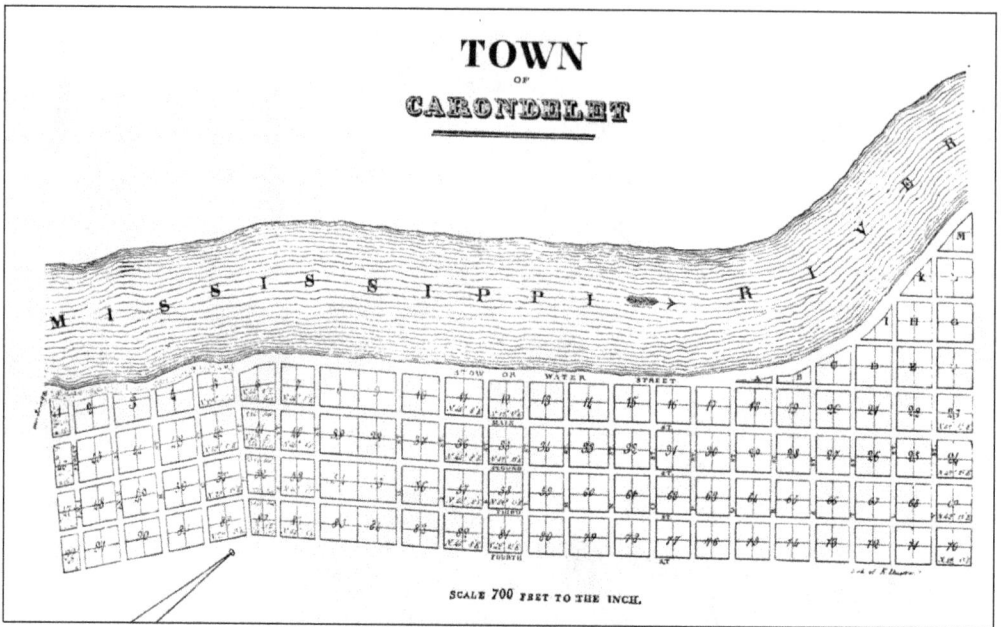

TOWN
OF
CARONDELET

SCALE 700 FEET TO THE INCH.

In 1851, the town of Carondelet was incorporated into a city and divided into three wards. The members of the first city council were Louis Teson, Wilson Primm, George F. Eichelberger, Jacob Stein, Charles Schirmer, and Napoleon B. Franklin. Their names indicate an ethnic change in the community from French to more of a German influence. The map above of the city shows the New Orleans–style layout of streets. (Courtesy of the Carondelet Historical Society.)

This is the common seal of the City of Carondelet, which is circular and no more than two inches in diameter. The words *en avant* on the seal accompanied by the female figure with an index finger of the right hand pointing forward is French for "forward." (Courtesy of the Carondelet Historical Society.)

Roswell M. Field, the attorney for Dred Scott, purchased property around the same time as Henry Taylor Blow and Wilson Primm on both sides of Loughborough Avenue. He later served as the city's attorney. (Courtesy of the Eugene Field House and Toy Museum.)

Field took on the legal battle of Dred Scott, an enslaved individual who lived in St. Louis and was taken by his owner to live in free territories. Upon his return to St. Louis, he sued to obtain freedom for himself and his wife, Harriet. He lost his case and the U.S. Supreme Court declared in 1857 that a slave had no legal rights to sue in court. The Scotts were later freed by Taylor Blow. The court's decision was one of the contributing factors that led to the Civil War. (Drawings from *Frank Leslie's Illustrated*.)

Rev. Moses Dickson, pastor of the Freedman's Church and School in Carondelet, was one of the key St. Louis figures in the Civil War. He was the organizer of a secret society called the Knights of Liberty, whose goal was to enlist and arm southern slaves for an insurrection to end slavery. He was ready to give the command to move forward in July 1857 but saw the war coming. In the meantime, he turned the Knights from insurrection to underground action. (Courtesy of John A. Wright Sr.)

Here are the ruins of the Freedman's Church and School in Carondelet, which was completed on September 1, 1869, and destroyed by fire on October 4, 1869. The church was constructed on land donated by Henry Taylor Blow. (Courtesy of James Brown.)

Ruins of Freedman's Church and School, Carondelet, Mo.

MOSES DICKSON, Pastor.

Corner Stone laid, May 27th, 1869.   Church completed, Sept. 1st, 1869.   Destroyed by Fire, Oct. 4th, 1869.

Cost of Building, $10,500.00   Ground Donated by Hon. Henry T. Blow.

In August 1861, James B. Eads, a successful St. Louis businessman, leased the Carondelet Marine Railway to build ironclad gunboats for the Union. With a strong belief in his idea and backing from Pres. Abraham Lincoln's attorney general Edward Bates, Eads submitted a bid. Winning with the lowest bid and earliest delivery date, Eads began his work, delivering the first ironclad gunboat, the *St. Louis*, only two days after the promised delivery date. (Courtesy of the Carondelet Historical Society.)

This is the iron-covered *Carondelet*, a wooden steam-powered paddle wheeler that took part in a number of battles and played a major role in the siege of Vicksburg. The *Daily Missouri Republican*, on October 23, 1861, reported that James B. Eads had 560 employed on four boats that would soon be launched and put into the water. (Courtesy of the Carondelet Historical Society.)

Ulysses S. Grant, a West Point graduate, pictured here in his early career, was once a deliveryman in Carondelet who cut and delivered firewood to area families. He rose to the rank of general and was commander of the Union armies during the Civil War and later president of the United States. (Courtesy of Marc E. Kollbaum of the St. Louis Parks Department at Jefferson Barracks.)

John Stevens Bowen of Carondelet wore the Union uniform before he joined the Confederate Missouri 2nd Regiment. Grant defeated Bowen's Union army at Vicksburg. Rather than imprisoning the captured Confederates, he allowed them paroles. Before leaving Vicksburg, Bowen fell ill with dysentery. Grant offered him medical care, but he refused and died outside Raymond, Mississippi. (Courtesy of the Carondelet Historical Society.)

Brevet Brig. Gen. Madison Miller, the former mayor of Carondelet, is pictured here in full uniform. He was promoted to brevet brigadier general on March 13, 1865, for "gallant and meritorious services in the battle of Shiloh," where he was captured and thought dead by some. He was successful in Missouri in both politics and business. He was president of the Mountain Railroad and elected to the general assembly. (Courtesy of the Carondelet Historical Society.)

James Milton Turner (the son of John Turner, a free African American who worked as a veterinarian in Carondelet) was with Miller at the Battle of Shiloh. Not knowing Miller had been taken captive, he gave Miller up for being dead. He brought Miller's belongings back to Carondelet to his family, only later to discover he was still alive. Turner went on to become America's first African American diplomat when he became minister to Liberia and was a leader in the movement to establish schools in Missouri for African Americans. (Courtesy of the Callaway County Historical Society.)

ST. LOUIS
AND
IRON MOUNTAIN R.R.

ONLY RAILROAD TO SOUTH-EAST MISSOURI.

The Greatest Mineral Region in the World!

ONE DAILY PASSENGER TRAIN
FROM ST. LOUIS TO

POTOSI and PILOT KNOB

ONE DAILY TRAIN
FROM AND TO

De Soto and Intermediate Stations.

TEN DAILY TRAINS

BETWEEN CARONDELET AND ST. LOUIS

Connecting three times daily with Jefferson Barracks and Quarantine.

The Managers of this Railway endeavor to make it in all respects a first-class road, by continually adding new improvements for the accommodation of Passengers; and, from this fact, as well as from its low fare, and the beautiful scenery and rich mines along its course, this Railroad is not only the most popular route for pleasure excursions, but will invite a rapid increase of population, affording splendid opportunities for the location of country residences, villas, orchards, and other improvements.

S. D. BARLOW,
President and Superintendent.

ISIDOR BUSH,
General Freight and Passenger Agent.

In 1855, workmen laid the train tracks for the Iron Mountain Railroad between Arsenal Street and Carondelet with full service starting in 1858. Carondelet stations were at Elwood and Krauss Streets, Robert Avenue, and the dry docks. The commuter trip from St. Louis to the Elwood station took 40 minutes with 10 trains operating daily. In 1859, a large number of machine shops were built in Carondelet, employing more than 500 employees. (Courtesy of the Carondelet Historical Society.)

The Carondelet Marine and Dock (pictured here), along with the Iron Mountain Railroad, brought a great deal of employment to the community, which spurred on a rapid amount of growth in lodging houses and inns to serve workers. (Courtesy of the Carondelet Historical Society.)

The city began to prosper after the opening of the Iron Mountain Railroad route from St. Louis to Carondelet. At that point, it became necessary to move city hall in 1862 to Lafayette Hall, pictured here, at the southeast corner of South Broadway and Loughborough Avenue, over the objections of some residents. The hall was used by the city until 1870, when it was converted to commercial uses, which continued until 1949, when it was destroyed by fire. (Courtesy of the Carondelet Historical Society.)

A group of citizens, led by Henry Taylor Blow, initiated action that resulted in the construction of Carondelet's first regular school, pictured above in 1866, on the west side of Virginia Avenue south of Loughborough Avenue. The school was named Blow School in honor of Henry Taylor Blow, who played a major role in its establishment by contributing $500 of the $8,000 needed for construction. (Courtesy of the Carondelet Historical Society.)

30

Since Carondelet residents were mostly Catholic, their children went to the parish schools until 1866, with the city trustees authorizing the payment to the parishes for their education. A number of students attended St. Joseph's Academy, which was founded in 1841 as a boarding school and day school with the aid of Elizabeth Brown Mullanphy, wife of Judge John Mullanphy. The academy was chartered by the State of Missouri in 1853. (Courtesy of the Carondelet Historical Society.)

St. Joseph's Academy offered a wide variety of subjects to its students. This picture was taken in the painting studio. (Courtesy of the Carondelet Historical Society.)

The cornerstone for St. Boniface Church, pictured here, was laid on May 8, 1860. It was the first German parish in Carondelet. The church later established St. Boniface Hospital in 1873, which was later destroyed by fire. The patients were moved to Gillick's Hall at Michigan Avenue and Stein Street and later to several other locations until 1892, when a building was constructed at Grand Boulevard and Chippewa Street. (Courtesy of the Carondelet Historical Society.)

The St. Boniface parish founded its parish school in 1910. The school later moved to a new facility in 1949, which is now closed. Pictured here is a 1910 class at the school. (Courtesy of the Carondelet Historical Society.)

SS. Mary and Joseph Parish, at 6304 Minnesota Avenue, dates back to 1767 when a plot of ground was set aside for a parish church. The first church was erected in 1818 on this site with material from the old St. Louis Cathedral. In 1835, the original log church was replaced with a larger building of hewed wood. In 1841, the parish was named Mount Carmel, then changed to SS. Mary and Joseph. (Courtesy of the Carondelet Historical Society.)

After the Civil War, African Americans moved to Carondelet seeking employment in the growing Carondelet economy, living scattered throughout the community. The African American population reached its peak in 1920 at 1,063. Pictured here are members of the Albert Jefferson family. Albert, on the far right, was the first African American mail carrier in Carondelet. (Courtesy of the Carondelet Historical Society.)

These African Americans are pictured outside St. John's Methodist Church, constructed in 1869 on land donated by Henry Taylor Blow. It was the first African American church in Carondelet. (Courtesy of the Carondelet Historical Society.)

Three

EARLY SCHOOLS, CHURCHES, AND INSTITUTIONS

On April 4, 1870, the Carondelet City Council held its last meeting, and on the following day, by an act of the Missouri legislature, the City of St. Louis annexed Carondelet. With the annexation came many of the urban amenities of St. Louis. The St. Louis public schools, park, and library services expanded into the community as well as the services of the fire and police departments. New homes, churches, and institutions began to be constructed, and Carondelet began to take on a new look, while retaining much of its old St. Louis character. (Courtesy of the Carondelet Historical Society.)

The first police station to serve the Carondelet area opened in 1875 at Pennsylvania and Robert Avenues, just five years after Carondelet became a part of the city of St. Louis. This facility was used until 1931 when it was replaced by a new facility at the northeast corner of Kansas and Colorado Avenues. After the new construction, the old building was used as a distribution center for food and clothing during the Great Depression. (Courtesy of the Carondelet Historical Society.)

Members of the early police department are pictured outside the police station. (Courtesy of the Carondelet Historical Society.)

These early officers are dressed much better than their earlier counterparts of 1865, who wore blue flannel blouses that went to four inches above the knee with a standing collar one and a half inches high and an adornment of four silver-plated buttons. The men also received two pairs of brown pantaloons and a cap with an attached silver star. (Courtesy of the Carondelet Historical Society.)

Pictured here are some members of the volunteer fire department posing with their horse-drawn fire equipment in front of the station house in 1909. The water supply was furnished by a series of cisterns and wells. These were dug solely for this purpose and located at six intersections along Fourth Street (Michigan Avenue) and capped by stone lids. (Courtesy of the Carondelet Historical Society.)

The earliest form of public transportation between St. Louis and Carondelet was the horse-drawn omnibus with the first horsecar line starting in 1860 on Broadway and Michigan Avenue. It failed because it encompassed a greater area than the number of riders it attracted. Another line was inaugurated in May 1875 with connections made to a line into St. Louis. (Courtesy of the Carondelet Historical Society.)

The electric streetcar was introduced in 1891 and served the area until the 1950s when motor buses were substituted. (Courtesy of the Carondelet Historical Society.)

The Blow School soon became inadequate to serve the growing number of students in the community. Through the efforts of Dr. Max Starkloff and his colleagues, Carondelet School was constructed in the southern part of the community in 1871, at 8221 Minnesota Avenue, at an estimated cost of $35,000. There were no drinking fountains in the hall, and students had to go to the basement for a drink using a dipper to take water from a bucket. The rooms were lit with coal oil lamps and heated with wood and coal stoves. (Courtesy of the Carondelet Historical Society.)

Pictured here is an early kindergarten class outside the Carondelet School with its teacher and school administrator. (Courtesy of the Carondelet Historical Society.)

Susan Blow, the daughter of Henry Taylor Blow, after returning from Europe and observing a German kindergarten developed by Fredrich Froebel, encouraged St. Louis Public School superintendent Dr. William Torrey Harris to open an experimental kindergarten. This was the beginning of the kindergarten program in St. Louis and America. (Courtesy of the Carondelet Historical Society.)

This is Des Peres School, where Susan Blow started the now famous kindergarten program, as it appeared in 1876. (Courtesy of the Carondelet Historical Society.)

This picture was taken of Susan Blow's first kindergarten class at Des Peres School while students were engaged in one of their many activities. The idea of the kindergarten program was to help develop children's minds under six and prepare them for learning. During classes, the students worked with bright colored material and learning activities to stimulate their minds. (Courtesy of the Carondelet Historical Society.)

The students pictured here are taking part in a gardening activity that was part of the kindergarten program. (Courtesy of the Carondelet Historical Society.)

The Vulcan Corporation's new plant in 1872 brought a large number of a new immigrant population, Irish, to the community. This prompted Archbishop Peter Kenrick to establish St. Columbkille's Church, pictured here that same year. After the plant closed, the Irish population declined, and the church was closed in 1952. (Courtesy of the Carondelet Historical Society.)

Pictured here is a 1907 class at St. Columbkille. The school was located on the first floor of the facility and the church on the second. In 1950, the archdiocese warned St. Columbkille that the school was inadequate, in violation of safety codes, and would have to be closed down. In a short time, the church and school were closed and vanquished shortly by wreckers, taking with them an important part of history. (Courtesy of the Carondelet Historical Society.)

Carondelet opened its first school for African Americans, Public School No. 6, at Virginia Avenue and Bowen Street in 1873, in response to a state law requiring segregated schools. The school was later named for Martin R. Delaney, an African American publisher and physician. The school was razed in 1911, when a new school was constructed. (Courtesy of the Carondelet Historical Society.)

The Delaney School band, pictured here, was one of the first bands, black or white, in the St. Louis public schools. The band was organized in 1912 by Robert Johnson, a mason. This picture was taken in 1916 at 6106 Colorado Avenue in front of the home of Charles Brown Sr. (Courtesy of James Brown.)

Once the African American students completed their elementary education, they had to travel into downtown St. Louis by public transit for high school until 1954. This picture is of Sumner High School at its second location at Fifteenth and Walnut Streets in downtown St. Louis. Sumner opened in 1874 and is the oldest high school west of the Mississippi River for African American students. (Courtesy of Julia Davis.)

Members of Sumner High School's first football team are pictured here, with Carondelet resident Virgil McKnight Sr. in the second row, second from the left. (Courtesy of Sumner High School.)

St. Rita's Academy at 4650 South Broadway was an African American girls' school run by the Oblate Sisters of Providence, a religious order founded in 1829 in Baltimore, Maryland. The sisters moved to this site in 1921. This academy and boarding school provided lodging for girls in grades 7 through 12, with a few day students. The property was used until 1950 and sold in 1958. (Courtesy of the Midwest Jesuit Archives.)

The school curriculum was similar to that of most private girls' schools of the time. It included algebra, geometry, Latin, French, biology, chemistry, and religion. Music lessons were available, and etiquette also was included in the curriculum. (Courtesy of the Midwest Jesuit Archives.)

Pictured here is the third Blow school on this site. This Flemish Renaissance architectural–style building was designed by William B. Ittner. The first building was constructed in 1866 and the second building in 1883, each razed to make way for the other. (Courtesy of the Carondelet Historical Society.)

This early picture of Blow students shows them involved in a hallway exercise. (Courtesy of the Carondelet Historical Society.)

An early-1900s female Blow staff is pictured here outside the building with the school principal. (Courtesy of the Carondelet Historical Society.)

As the community continued to grow, the St. Louis Board of Education found a need to construct Lyons Elementary School at 7417 Vermont Avenue. The school was named for Nathaniel Lyon, a Union general in the Civil War. An early graduation class is pictured here outside the school. (Courtesy of the Carondelet Historical Society.)

Woerner Elementary School at 6131 Leona Street was constructed in 1931 to serve the students in the southwestern part of the community. The school was named to honor lawyer and judge J. Gabriel Woerner. (Courtesy of the Carondelet Historical Society.)

Woerner Elementary School had a number of activities for students as well as parents. The school cheerleaders and majorettes are pictured here in front of the school in the 1940s. (Courtesy of the Carondelet Historical Society.)

This school at 6138 Virginia Avenue, first known as Delaney School, was constructed to serve the community's African American population in 1911. When its student population declined, it was turned over to the white students and renamed Maddox School to honor John A. J. Maddox, an assistant superintendent of schools. The school has since been developed into condominiums. (Courtesy of the Carondelet Historical Society.)

This 1920s graduating class is posed outside the Woodward school at 725 Bellerive Boulevard, which was constructed in 1921 to serve the students in the Bellerive area. (Courtesy of the Carondelet Historical Society.)

The white students in Carondelet, upon the completion of elementary school, traveled to Cleveland High School, at 4352 Louisiana Avenue, which was completed in 1915. They were joined by the community's African American students after 1954. Prior to the construction of Cleveland High School, white students traveled to Central High School in north St. Louis. (Courtesy of the Carondelet Historical Society.)

One of Central's early football teams is pictured here. The two young men in the center, John Samb and Bob Kinsey, are from Carondelet. (Courtesy of the Carondelet Historical Society.)

For young ladies seeking a life of dedicated service as nuns, the sisters of St. Joseph Convent, at 6400 Minnesota Avenue, provided them an opportunity. The Sisters of St. Joseph of Carondelet have played a valuable role in the community since settling in the area in 1836. (Courtesy of the Sisters of St. Joseph of Carondelet Archives.)

A class of young ladies is pictured here as it prepares to take its vows. (Courtesy of the Sisters of St. Joseph of Carondelet Archives.)

Carondelet-Markham Memorial Church can trace its history back to 1849, when meetings were held in a vacant room in the home of Gen. Madison Miller at the foot of Bowen Street. Construction began on a new church on this site in 1859 but was delayed because of the Civil War. The present church was built next to this old structure in 1896. (Photograph by John A. Wright Sr.)

Mellow Memorial Methodist Church, at 6701 Virginia Avenue, was organized in 1857 as the Carondelet Methodist Church. The first church on the site was dedicated on May 17, 1857, and the present building in 1904. The church was constructed with bricks from the old building at a cost of $22,000, including furnishings. In 1941, the name of the church was changed to Mellow Memorial Methodist Church to honor the Thomas Mellow family. (Photograph by John A. Wright Sr.)

Carondelet Baptist Church, at Virginia and Robert Avenues, was organized in 1867 as the First Baptist Church of Carondelet. Its first building was dedicated in 1872, at Fifth and Taylor Streets. The church moved to its present location in 1928 and constructed a new school and gymnasium in 1954 adjacent to the church. (Courtesy of the Carondelet Historical Society.)

Mount Zion Methodist Church at the northeast corner of Virginia and Koehn Avenues, which was founded in 1894, provided an educational program for elementary age students at its location. (Courtesy of the Carondelet Historical Society.)

St. Paul's Protestant Episcopal Church, at 6518 Michigan Avenue, was founded in 1868. The members held services in rented quarters until the church was completed in 1870. A stone in the front yard marks the point of the beginning of the original survey of the Spanish grant to the inhabitants of the village of Carondelet. (Photograph by John A. Wright Sr.)

St. Trinity Lutheran Church, at Vermont Avenue and Koeln Street, was organized in the 1850s by German farmers and craftsmen. In March 1872, the community incorporated as the German Evangelical Lutheran Sanctus Trinitatis Congregation. The building pictured here with members in front was dedicated in June 1893. The original tower of the church was the tallest in Carondelet until the tornado of May 27, 1896. (Courtesy of the Carondelet Historical Society.)

This church, now known as the Church of the Nazarene at 7100 Virginia Avenue, was constructed in 1890 and has served as the home of the Carondelet Methodist Church. It later changed hands to Jesuits and became the Parish of Our Lady of Covadonga, being established as a mission for Spanish Catholics in the area. It has been the home of the Church of the Nazarene for nearly 70 years. (Courtesy of the Carondelet Historical Society.)

The members of Corinthian Missionary Baptist Church at 6326 Colorado Avenue can trace their roots back to 1875 when Rev. George W. West came to Carondelet to establish a church. At that time, prayer meetings were held in the home of Richard Walker. The group formed the Second Baptist Church and moved to Krauss Street. The church built this frame building in 1895. (Courtesy of Corinthian Missionary Baptist Church.)

This three-story structure at 6818 Michigan Avenue, known as the South End Masonic Temple, was completed in 1907. It was the home of the Good Hope Lodge, Cache Lodge, Venus Chapter, and Odd Fellows and served as a meeting place for a number of community organizations and groups. (Courtesy of Carondelet Historical Society.)

On May 30, 1881, the Odd Fellows of Carondelet, along with community residents and leaders, gathered for the dedication of the Odd Fellows Cemetery at 9950 South Broadway. The lot had been purchased for a lodge hall and was dedicated as a place for the burial of Odd Fellow members and their family and friends. (Courtesy of the Carondelet Historical Society.)

Jefferson Barracks National Cemetery was established in the Carondelet Commons in 1863. It was an extension of the Old Post Cemetery at Jefferson Barracks, which was established just 13 months after the establishment of Jefferson Barracks in 1826. There are over 103,000 men and women buried in the cemetery, including more than 12,000 Union and 1,000 Confederate victims of the Civil War. (Courtesy of the Carondelet Historical Society.)

Jefferson Barracks was the burial grave site for some Native Americans. These Native Americans are gathered at a grave site in 1914 to pay tribute to a hero. (Courtesy of the Carondelet Historical Society.)

The Altenheim was established in 1899 when prominent members of the German community came together to form the Altenheim Society, for the care of the elderly. The agency purchased the 15-room home of Charles P. Chouteau on May 11, 1901. Through the years, many additions and changes have been made to the original structure, until it was razed in 1972 to make way for a six-story residential building. (Courtesy of the Carondelet Historical Society.)

This is the St. Joseph Orphan Asylum for boys, established in 1846 for boys in downtown St. Louis, in 1900. In 1895, this forerunner of the St. Joseph's Home moved its operations to 4701 South Grand Boulevard. (Courtesy of the Carondelet Historical Society.)

These young eighth-grade ladies from Blow Elementary School were members of the Alcott Reading Club, founded in 1905 by Lillian Evans just before the Carondelet Library opened. They are, from left to right, (first row) Marie Kammerer, Carrie McFadden, and Alice Doering; (second row) Mabel Doering, Helen Bribach, Hazel Etling, and Margaret Evans. (Courtesy of the Carondelet Historical Society.)

The Carondelet branch of the public library at 6800 Michigan Avenue was completed in 1908 at a cost of $73,000 from the Andrew Carnegie Fund. Interested citizens raised $4,500 for the library site. The building is considered by some to be an excellent example of Greek Ionic architecture. (Courtesy of the Carondelet Historical Society.)

Members of the Spanish community dedicated this building, known as the Spanish Society, at 7107 Michigan Avenue in 1937. The Spanish residents had come to Carondelet in the early 1900s to work at the Edgar Zinc Company, and their numbers declined after the plant moved in 1921. Activities are still conducted at the facility with membership open to all who share the same mission as the society. (Courtesy of the Carondelet Historical Society.)

Members of the Spanish Society are posed in front of their new headquarters on Michigan Avenue in 1938. The society was organized to promote Spanish culture and tradition. (Courtesy of the Spanish Society.)

60

Four

COMMUNITY SERVICES, BUSINESSES, AND INDUSTRIES

Business and industry has been an important part of the life of the Carondelet community since its early beginning. Early settlers raised their own livestock and grew and harvested the fields. As the area developed, the need developed for businesses to serve the population. One of the earlier entrepreneurs was Christian Hoffmeister, who opened a livery stable at 7800 Main Street (South Broadway) in 1858. When the need grew for public transportation, he established and began operation of the St. Louis and Carondelet Omnibus Line. After the Civil War, he branched into the funeral business and became the area's first funeral director. (Courtesy of the Carondelet Historical Society.)

The general store was the mainstay of the community. It sold everything from tools for everyday use to food for daily use. There was a time when sugar sold for 24 pounds for $1, green coffee for 10¢ a pound, and cereals such as hominy, cornmeal, rolled oats, and rice came in barrels. (Courtesy of the Carondelet Historical Society.)

Carondelet was once the home of several cigar factories. Workers are pictured here outside the M. Hammer and Company Cigar Manufactory. Jos. Menendez was the last maker of hand-rolled cigars in the area. A 1962 newspaper article in St. Louis commented on the fact that brewery workers smoked the same cigars as lawyers. (Courtesy of the Carondelet Historical Society.)

Members of the Bailey Dairy are gathered in preparation for their deliveries. In the early days of the community, milk was delivered by a horse-drawn wagon. A horse and wagon were also an important part of the grocery business, due to the fact that homes were not equipped with telephones. Drivers were often asked to deliver packages after dropping off the groceries. (Courtesy of the Carondelet Historical Society.)

Carondelet News.

Vol. V. No. 18   South St. Louis, Mo., Saturday, January 7, 1905. $1.00 a Year in Advance.

THOMAS GAVIN KILLED.

FORMER DETECTIVE'S LIFE ENDED BY WATCHMAN'S BULLET

BUSINESS MEN'S MEETING.

CROSSLEY IN TROUBLE.

STOLE A SKIRT.

CHARLES BRUNO DEAD.

COLUMBIA STAR MILLING COMPANY.

❖ THE BEST FLOUR ❖

PACKED IN

THE BEST SACK.

Every Sack Guaranteed to be the Best.

FOR SALE BY ALL LEADING GROCERS.

Phones: Bell South 145-M; Kinloch Victor 532.

GAS COKE

LUMP - AND - CRUSHED

Coal, Lime, Sand, Sewer Pipe

PORTLAND AND LOUISVILLE CEMENTS

Over the years, the Carondelet community has been served by several newspapers: the *Carondelet News Era, St. Louis Times, Bugle,* and *Neighborhood Link News*. The *Carondelet News*, pictured here, was published on Saturdays, from about 1900 to 1930, with B. F. Gillreath as editor. (Courtesy of the Carondelet Historical Society.)

Klausmann's Brewery was established in 1878 and had a thriving business until Prohibition. The brewery was comprised of a complex of stone and brick buildings modeled after the breweries of Germany. After the beer was produced, it was taken to local merchants by horse-drawn wagon. In 1902, the brewery had 120 employees. The brewery was torn down in 1937. (Courtesy of the Carondelet Historical Society.)

The old Carondelet Mill, at 7020 South Broadway, was built in 1867. It was conveniently located close to the river for easy shipping and near farmers, making it unnecessary for them to travel to St. Louis. It was razed in 1956. (Courtesy of the Carondelet Historical Society.)

Southern Commercial and Savings Bank was organized in 1891 by John Krauss and opened for business with $100,000 in capital. Krauss also served as the bank's first president. The bank's first home was located at 7129 South Broadway at Nagel Street. (Courtesy of the Carondelet Historical Society.)

Pictured here is Mueller's grocery store at 7229 South Broadway, which had a series of doors that could be opened in warm weather, making it a somewhat open-air store. It had a second story with a porch that extended over the sidewalk. (Courtesy of the Carondelet Historical Society.)

W. J. Schneider poses in the doorway of his pharmacy at 6343 Michigan Avenue in the early 1900s. A 1966 publication listed other stores owned by Wailbel, Widmann, Winkelmann, Zeller, Nitzschmann, Guelker, and Brown in the community. (Courtesy of the Carondelet Historical Society.)

This typical mid-19th-century vernacular brick row–trimmed store building at 7102–7129 South Broadway is a fine example of buildings where the owner or tenants lived above shops on the first floor. (Courtesy of the Carondelet Historical Society.)

African Americans owned a number of businesses along South Broadway, Colorado Avenue, and Iron Street. Some of the businesses identified in early city directories include Britton and McKnight's Barbershop at 6311 South Broadway, Major Brown's Barbershop at 700 South Broadway, Eliza Shores Dressmaking Shop at 7008 South Broadway Boulevard, and Purnell's Ice and Coal Company at 6105 Colorado Avenue. (Courtesy of Verna Murphy.)

This interior photograph of Koenig Brothers Market, at 7103 South Broadway, was taken in 1939. Pictured from left to right are Edward Steiner, Raoul Campa, Albert Koen, Ollie Fisher, and Joseph Koenig. The Koenig Brothers Market served the community for a number of years prior to its closing. (Courtesy of the Carondelet Historical Society.)

It was the immigrant population that supplied the needed labor to produce the goods demanded by a developing country. They came from Germany, Spain, and Italy to Carondelet. Antonio Villa is pictured on the right with his wife, Margarite. They immigrated to Carondelet from a suburb of Milan in 1898. He got a job in the Missouri Blasting Mill, located at South Broadway and Holly Hills Avenue. Antonio was the father of Albert "Red" Villa and grandfather of state representative Tom Villa. Tom Villa's other grandparents, pictured on the left, John and Rose Spesia, moved to the community in the early 1900s. (Courtesy of Tom Villa.)

The steel mills and foundries in Carondelet were among the major employers of the community. These companies mostly were along South Broadway and brought a great deal of revenue to the community through such employers as Liberty Foundry, which employed 275; National Lead, employing 1,500; Semi-Steel Casting Company, 160; St. Louis Steel Casting, 225; and Hydraulic Brick Company, 550. (Courtesy of the Carondelet Historical Society.)

One of the many companies that moved to Carondelet during the early 1900s was Phelan-Faust Paint Manufacturing Company. The company moved to 932 Loughborough Avenue from East St. Louis, Illinois, in 1925. It manufactured all types of coating and protective finishes and employed about 225 workers. (Courtesy of the Carondelet Historical Society.)

As the population continued to grow, the farmland and nurseries slowly disappeared. Pictured here is John Knoll with his wife and one of his sons outside their greenhouse and nursery at the southwest corner of Kansas (Holly Hills) and Idaho Avenues. The Knolls sold some of their flowers from their horse-drawn wagon. Three of Knoll's sons became successful florists. (Courtesy of the Carondelet Historical Society.)

The Bevo Mill Restaurant, a longtime favorite in the Carondelet Commons on Gravois Avenue and Morganford Road, was built by August A. Busch Sr. in 1917. To develop his plans, Busch traveled to Europe to study windmills. According to stories, the rock for the construction was brought to the site by Busch's chauffeur in his Pierce-Arrow. During the process, two or three Pierce-Arrows were worn out. (Courtesy of the Carondelet Historical Society.)

The Carondelet Post Office has been a longtime fixture in the community. These men are posed outside the Carondelet station at 6924 South Broadway. (Courtesy of the Carondelet Historical Society.)

The St. Louis public schools for years operated a greenhouse a couple blocks south of Carondelet Park on 11.9 acres at Field and Blow Avenues. The greenhouse complex provided over 400 varieties of flowers and shrubbery for the schools. The greenhouse was also used for class instruction and field trips for students and teachers. (Courtesy of the Carondelet Historical Society.)

Pictured here is one of the floral displays at the St. Louis Board of Education greenhouse. The greenhouse opened around 1933, but the landscaping program began in the early 1900s. With the construction of a number of new schools, the district found it more cost-effective to grow its own plants. (Courtesy of the Carondelet Historical Society.)

One of the oldest fixtures in the area was the city workhouse at 4200 South Broadway, which was constructed in 1853. Men and women were sent here to work off their fines. In the 1960s, the rate was $3 per day. At that time, the daily cost per capita was $1.55 per inmate with that figure being reduced to $1.31 because of services performed by prisoners. (Courtesy of the Carondelet Historical Society.)

Many of the men at the workhouse worked in the rock quarry on the property where they broke big rocks into small ones that were sold and used by the city for various projects. Nearby residents always complained about the blasting in the quarry and the impact it had on their homes and property values. (Courtesy of the Carondelet Historical Society.)

For years, the four-story Carondelet Hotel in the 7200 block of South Broadway was a welcoming sight for visitors. The hotel, built in the mid-1800s, was a substantial brick structure with a spacious dining room and 50 rooms that could accommodate 100 guests. It was located opposite the rail station and housed the Carondelet Post Office. (Courtesy of the Carondelet Historical Society.)

After the South Broadway Carondelet Hotel closed, another Carondelet Hotel opened in the 6800 block of Michigan Avenue across from the Carondelet branch of the St. Louis Public Library and is now closed. (Courtesy of the Carondelet Historical Society.)

This sheet of advertisements shows a small sampling of some of the many services that were once available from Carondelet business owners and merchants during the community's years of growth. (Courtesy of the Carondelet branch of the St. Louis Public Library.)

South Broadway in downtown Carondelet is pictured here during its heyday, when it was full of shops and businesses. Many of these shops and businesses went out of business during the 1960s, when Interstate 55 averted traffic away from South Broadway. (Courtesy of the Carondelet Historical Society.)

The Michigan Theatre at 7224 Michigan Avenue was just one of several theaters that once served the area. It was a place where one could once see a couple of movies, a chapter play, cartoon, and newsreel for a few cents. (Courtesy of the Carondelet Historical Society.)

Plans to build a bridge across the Mississippi River from Carondelet to Illinois began about 1869, but these plans were abandoned until a group of businessmen successfully promoted the Jefferson Barracks Bridge. The bridge was completed on December 9, 1944. During its first year of operation, there were 280,624 vehicles using the bridge. By 1950, the number had grown to 1,915,304. (Courtesy of the Carondelet Historical Society.)

The construction of the Jefferson Barracks Bridge brought an end to the Davis Street ferry, which began operation in the mid-1800s. The ferry is reported to have handled as many as 1,000 cars in a day, making 80 trips in 12 hours. It is also reported to have taken as many as 2,000 bingo ladies across the river and back. (Courtesy of the Carondelet Historical Society.)

Carondelet for years has had citizens interested in building a healthy and thriving community. One of the early groups was the Carondelet Business Men's Association, incorporated in 1906. The men are pictured here at their annual banquet in 1915. (Courtesy of the Carondelet Historical Society.)

Members of the Carondelet Improvement Association are shown with Miss Flame of 1959, Grace Ann Parshall, during one of its annual events. This organization's goal was to work to make Carondelet both a habitable and enjoyable place to live. Some of its credits include the Ivory Street underpass, attracting several manufacturing plants and businesses, and the consummation of the Jefferson Barracks project. (Courtesy of the Carondelet Historical Society.)

In the 1960s, Interstate 55 came through the community and averted traffic from the community's main shopping district on South Broadway, causing a dramatic loss of business. Through the efforts of organizations such as the Carondelet Community Betterment Federation and the South Broadway Merchants Association, the community is being revitalized and making a thriving recovery. (Photograph by John A. Wright Sr.)

The great flood of 1993 had a major impact on the downtown section of the community. It was one of the hardest-hit sections in St. Louis. This area has now made a comeback and is taking on a new and vibrant look. (Courtesy of the Carondelet Historical Society.)

Five

RECREATION, CELEBRATION, AND AMUSEMENT

Ever since its settlement, Carondelet has been a community known as a place for enjoyment and relaxation. Early in its history, it had the name of Vide Poche, French for "empty pocket." It was said residents from nearby towns would come to gamble and leave with empty pockets. Over the years, the residents have provided an array of activities through its institutions and community organizations. Carondelet Park is still the location for many organizational and family events. The three couples above are enjoying an afternoon on the ice in the park. (Courtesy of the Carondelet branch of the St. Louis Public Library.)

One of the enjoyable events of the warm months was a truck picnic. A large truck was rented from a local business for the day, and the young men and ladies would head for the Meramec River or Falling Springs in Illinois. Some of the clubs held a picnic every Sunday. (Courtesy of the Carondelet Historical Society.)

Pictured in the early 1900s, these young men are members of the Carondelet Motor Club, which was located on Schirmer Street and Michigan Avenue. With many of the streets unpaved, it was not always an easy task of getting around, but for the youth it was no doubt fun. The club members would often ride their bikes out into the woods and go camping. (Courtesy of the Carondelet Historical Society.)

Fishing was a favorite pastime for many in the Carondelet community. Many residents would travel to the Mississippi River's edge or to the Meramec River and River Des Peres or even to Falling Springs in Illinois. (Courtesy of the Carondelet Historical Society.)

Many residents would catch a boat at the Davis Street ferry landing and head across the river for a fun day of fishing or bingo or head down the river to Kimmswick for the day for 25¢. Those seeking a real vacation would take the *Delta Queen* for a two- or three-day trip for about $18. (Courtesy of the Carondelet Historical Society.)

A

Novel ✦ Entertainment

TURNER HALL,

Corner Michigan and Robert Aves.

Thursday Night, December 14, 1899.

PROGRAM.

ADMISSION, - 25 CENTS.

Performance at 8 O'Clock Sharp.

The young men in the town found Turner Hall at 7200 Michigan Avenue a great place to meet and let their hair down. Many gave dances to earn money to purchase things they wanted. (Courtesy of the Carondelet Historical Society.)

The 1934 Carondelet Division Baseball Championship was won by members of the Carondelet Spanish Society. The members of the society are strong supporters of baseball and soccer teams for their youth. They feel if young people are involved in sports and have strong family ties, they are less likely to become juvenile delinquents. (Courtesy of the Spanish Society.)

These young men are members of the Carondelet Germania Turnverein Drum Corps. The local German community organized the group in 1875 to develop programs to encourage intellectual pursuits and political involvement as well as health and exercise. Turnvereins supported and lobbied for physical education to be included in the public school curriculum. (Courtesy of the Carondelet Historical Society.)

The Carondelet Sangerbund, pictured here, was a very popular German singing group around the beginning of the 20th century that sponsored song festivals and musicals. (Courtesy of the Carondelet Historical Society.)

Musicals were not just confined to the men in the community. These women are members of the 1922 Woodward Elementary School kitchen band. They are, from left to right, (first row) ? Harbirieu, ? Kupfer, ? Webster, ? Mack, ? Sturn, ? Wagner, ? Schmidt, ? Wiler, ? Rowe, and ? Miselborn; (second row) ? Keisten, ? Peterwain, ? Pacben, ? Gaehl, ? Newbaver, ? Heichelbech, ? Maehl, ? Kalbrassen, ? Lund, and three unidentified women. (Courtesy of the Carondelet Historical Society.)

One of the early celebrations of St. Anthony parish was the Corpus Christi procession, which began in 1878. (Courtesy of the Carondelet Historical Society.)

These youngsters are taking part in the annual St. Boniface parade. During the spring of the year, many schools in the community would march from their school to Carondelet Park. (Courtesy of the Carondelet Historical Society.)

These participants are gathered in Meramec Park on May 5, 1917, to prepare for a balloon race. Participants were from a number of companies and businesses around the area. Balloon racing was a major sport during the early part of the 20th century. (Courtesy of the Carondelet Historical Society.)

These men are members of the Western Carondelet Rowing Club, which was located at 5000 South Broadway. This boat club, like the Century Boat Club, was comprised of professional men who rowed and raced on the Mississippi River. The Century Boat House later became the Edgewater Club and Restaurant. (Courtesy of the Carondelet Historical Society.)

Members of the Carondelet Women's Club, founded in 1901, are pictured here dressed in period clothing for one of its programs. The club was organized for social, cultural, and charitable purposes. The club met once a month at the Carondelet branch of the public library and sponsored musicals and dramatic programs based on Carondelet history. (Courtesy of the Carondelet branch of the St. Louis Public Library.)

These ladies are members of the Carondelet Heights Rod and Gun Club. This picture was taken in 1905 in Carondelet Park. (Courtesy of the Carondelet Historical Society.)

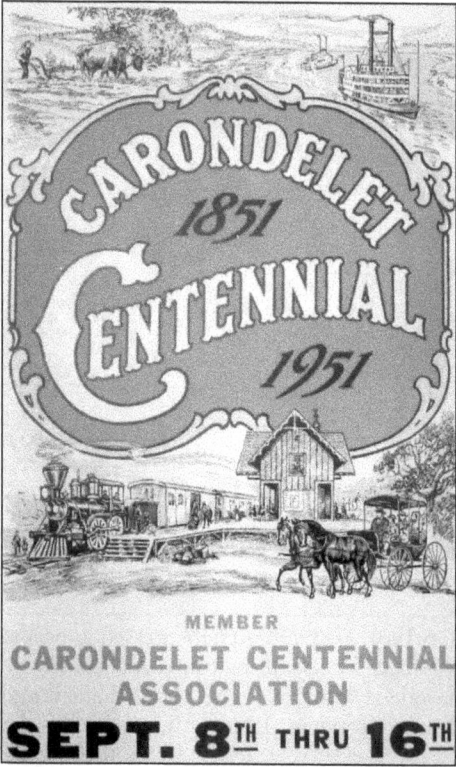

The 1951 Carondelet centennial was a major event in the community. Gov. Christopher Bond, Congresswoman Leonor K. Sullivan, Mayor John Poelker, and a host of dignitaries came out for the 100th birthday of the community. The celebration included a parade with marching bands, floats, and clowns. (Courtesy of the Carondelet Historical Society.)

Carondelet Days sponsored by the Carondelet Community Corporation in the 1970s did a great deal to develop community pride and a sense of place. It also brought many visitors to the area. (Courtesy of the Carondelet Historical Society.)

Along with the floats during the Carondelet centennial in 1951, a host of participants dressed in the costumes of the earlier days of the city and rode in vintage cars. (Courtesy of the Carondelet Historical Society.)

While celebrating the occasion, the planners allowed some African American students to voice their concerns about the St. Louis Board of Education closing their school and sending them across town for their education. (Courtesy of the Carondelet branch of the St. Louis Public Library.)

Carondelet Park has been considered an excellent place to spend an enjoyable summer evening since its early beginnings as a public park. These residents are enjoying a summer concert sponsored by Laclede Gas Company. (Courtesy of the Carondelet Historical Society.)

During the 1940s, Tom Thumb weddings were favorite events for many organizations. Some institutions used this event to raise money to support the war effort. These youngsters are members of Mellow Memorial Methodist Church. (Courtesy of the Carondelet Historical Society.)

In 1958, the Carondelet branch of the St. Louis Public Library celebrated its 50 years of service to the community. Members of the 50th Anniversary Steering Committee were Roger T. Moran, Elizabeth Golterman, Mrs. Lee Best, Mrs. Perley A. Dates, Prudencio Garcia, Frank K. Harris, Mildred Hayes, Claron B. Hutchison, George Meenan, Louis M. Nourse, Helen M. Riedckus, Mrs. Arthur O. Rosskopf, and A. C. Waldemar. (Courtesy of the Carondelet branch of the St. Louis Public Library.)

Carondelet resident Mayor Raymond R. Tucker is pictured here talking with one of the guests during the 50th anniversary celebration at the library. Tucker once worked in the library part-time while going to school, stacking books and doing other chores. (Courtesy of the Carondelet branch of the St. Louis Public Library.)

91

Baseball, soccer, bowling, and other team events have been a longtime part of the Carondelet community's recreational activities. These men are members of the 1936–1937 Carondelet Recreation Bowling League season. (Courtesy of the Carondelet Historical Society.)

Pictured here are members of Carondelet Sunday Morning Athletic Club's senior baseball team, which won the 1953 Southside Baseball Championship. The team members include Walter Rosech, Dick Tichaeck, Clarence Bauer, John Schaller, Ray Smerer, Jerry Cunningham, Al Repple, Bill Davis, Ed Albrecht (coach), Mike Waluski, Joe DiCarol, Bill Franz, Pat McGuire, Warren Stecher, Paul Diekes, Earl Kestler (coach), Monte Gummels (manager), and Lawrence Sartori (past club president). The batboys are Jimmy Gunmerls and Billy Gumnels. (Courtesy of the Carondelet Historical Society.)

Six

HOMES OF THE COMMUNITY

Founded in 1767, Carondelet history has been preserved in many homes and institutions dating back to the 1800s. One can still find a glimpse of the old river town as residents of Carondelet honor the past while building for the future. This home, at 6727 Michigan Avenue, has been inhabited since 1859 and once belonged to John Stevens Bowen, a Confederate army major general. Bowen organized the 1st Missouri Regiment, but the siege of Vicksburg left him very ill. When Ulysses S. Grant took the city, Bowen was paroled and died on the way to Raymond, Mississippi. His wife lived in the home after his death. (Courtesy of the Carondelet Historical Society.)

This French-style home, at Reilly Avenue and Primm Street on the northwest corner, was built for Alsatian-born Joseph Otgzenberger in 1858. It has an elevated gallery with stairs leading to the second-story entrance. The back entrance has the integration of the roof structure to the back porch in Alsatian building tradition. (Courtesy of the Carondelet Historical Society.)

German immigrants of the 1840s and 1850s built stone houses in this section of town known as Stein's Town. These stone row houses at 200 and 204 Stein Street were placed on the National Register of Historic Places on March 27, 1980. This four-house row was built around 1851 for Ignatz Uhrig, proprietor of the popular cave and brewery located at the southeast corner of Jefferson and Washington Avenues. These homes are one and a half stories in height and built close to the street. (Photograph by John A. Wright Sr.)

The Larry Simon house, at 5801 Minnesota Avenue, was constructed between 1857 and 1875. It lies just a few blocks east of the French village of Carondelet and is typical of the French Gothic style. The distinguishing features of this style are pointed-arched windows, steep roofs, and sidings with vertical boards overlapped with strips of wood. It is one of a very few pure French Gothic houses that can be found in the St. Louis area. (Courtesy of the Carondelet Historical Society.)

This is one of the several great bluff homes that once graced the landscape on South Broadway. This impressive home, at 5218 South Broadway, belonged to John Scullin of Scullin Steel. It was designed by George Pegram, who designed the union station in 1867. Missouri governor John S. Marmaduke also once occupied the home. It was wrecked in the 1940s. (Courtesy of the Carondelet Historical Society.)

Subdivisions are nothing new to the area. Developer John C. Ivory designed this one in the southern end of the city of Carondelet in 1855. (Courtesy of Jaymes Dearing.)

A desirable location for large homes was "upon the hill" along Michigan Avenue, which provided an excellent view of the river. These homes were on Michigan Avenue and Krauss Street. (Courtesy of the Carondelet Historical Society.)

Since the streets were unpaved, the city provided the services of workers to dampen the streets to keep down dust. (Courtesy of the Carondelet Historical Society.)

This Empire-style home at 6622 Michigan Avenue was built about 1865. The original owner is unknown. (Photograph by John A. Wright Sr.)

In the early days of Carondelet, the area in which this house stands at 7012 Minnesota Avenue was known as the common fields. This home was built in the early 1840s with stones from the quarry between Reilly and Polk Avenues. In the 1850s, the present front of the house was the back. Since no home stood to the east, it provided a beautiful view of the river. It has 12 rooms with two attic rooms. The basement contains a kitchen on both sides. (Photograph by John A. Wright Sr.)

These shops at 7121–7129 South Broadway are typical of mid-19th-century vernacular brick row–trimmed buildings with stone and wrought iron. The owners or tenants lived above the shops on the first floor. The building was constructed in 1879 and was the first home of Southern Commercial and Savings Bank in 1891. (Photograph by John A. Wright Sr.)

The Johnstons built this home in 1928 at 521 Loughborough Avenue, where they lived for 77 years. This apartment coincides with the Flemish Renaissance architectural style of Blow School and the Carondelet branch of the YMCA across the street. James Johnston was the first president of Tin Foil and Metal Company in Carondelet. (Photograph by John A. Wright Sr.)

The 1920s saw the construction of these homes along Bellerive Boulevard, thought by some to have been influenced by the arts and crafts movement. This movement came out of late-19th-century England, where it was felt simplicity, beauty, and fine craftsmanship should work together. (Photograph by John A. Wright Sr.)

The 1920s with the Hollywood rage brought on the development of Holly Hills, "the California of St. Louis." Its developer, William A. Federer, felt a little of Hollywood's glamour would rub off on the development. He wanted the homes to reflect English estate homes, German castles, and country cottages. The first building permits were issued by the city in 1926. (Courtesy of the Carondelet Historical Society.)

Seven

CARONDELET TODAY

Carondelet is known as one of St. Louis's best-kept secrets. The community's parks, historic buildings, renovations, and new construction offer something to meet every need. Major developments in the making include the 40-acre office warehouse project at the coke and coal gasification plant site and the $350 million casino in the Carondelet Commons. Thanks to the efforts of the Carondelet Historical Society, founded in 1966; the South Broadway Merchants Association, organized in 1971; and the Carondelet Community Betterment Federation, incorporated in 1973, the community moves onward and upward. Organizing officers of the Carondelet Historical Society are pictured here with St. Louis mayor A. J. Cervantes. (Courtesy of the Carondelet Historical Society.)

The Sisters of St. Joseph of Carondelet and the motherhouse, pictured here at 6400 Minnesota Avenue, have served the community since 1836. In keeping with their beliefs, they continue to invite guests of all faiths who seek to work and live in harmony with the mission of the sisters. Their facility is open for meetings and retreats. (Courtesy of the Sisters of St. Joseph of Carondelet Archives.)

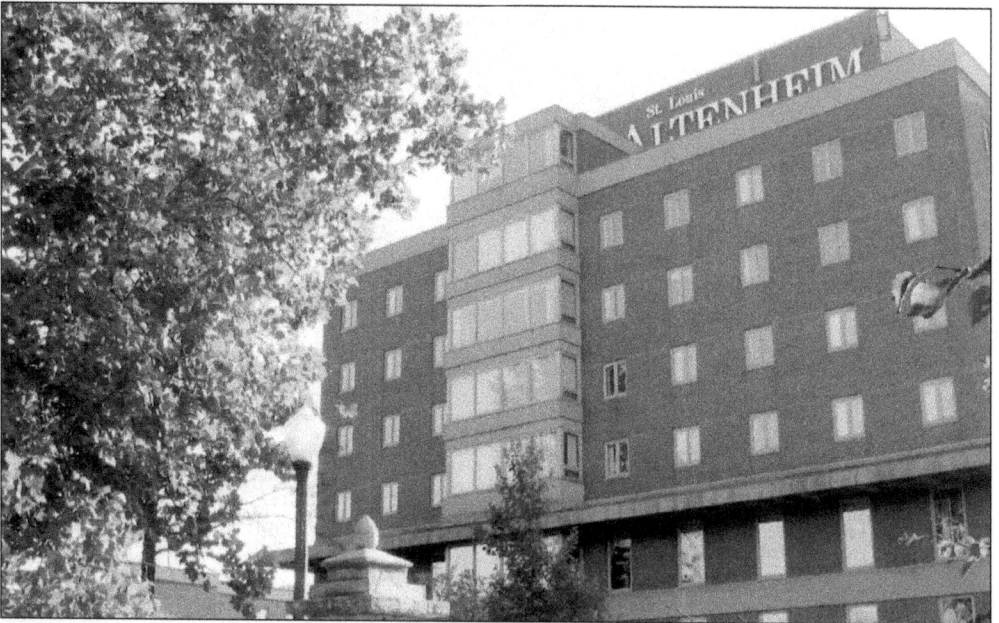

The Altenheim (aged persons home), organized in the late 1800s, has been home for many of the community residents during their later years. It moved to its present location at 5405 South Broadway in 1901, when it purchased the home of Charles P. Chouteau. Through the years, many changes and additions have been made to the building. The high-rise addition seen here was added in the late 1960s. (Photograph by John A. Wright Sr.)

The Carondelet Community Betterment Federation was formed in 1971 to address the problems and needs of the Carondelet neighborhood, to seek solutions and services for residents, and to work with other organizations to avoid duplication of services. Today the agency continues to provide an array of services through its office at 6408 Michigan Avenue, aimed at community improvement and development. (Photograph by John A. Wright Sr.)

Health care is within the reach of all residents at the Family Care Health Center at 401 Holly Hills Avenue. The center was founded in 1969 with the goal of decreasing the infant mortality rate and to provide primary health care services for uninsured and underinsured people in south St. Louis. Today the center provides affordable and accessible services to anyone from this new $6.9 million facility. (Photograph by John A. Wright Sr.)

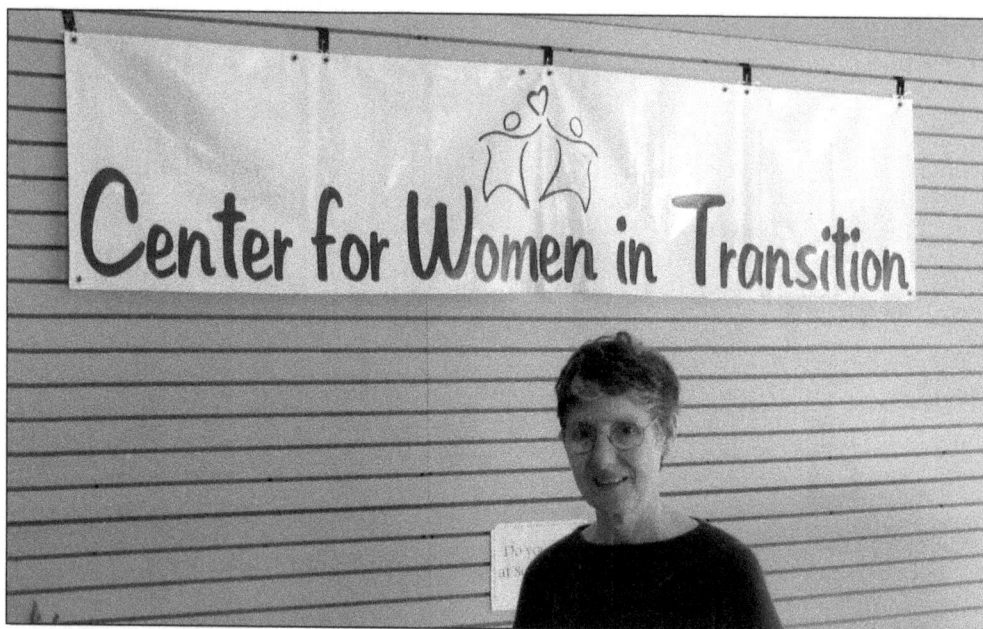

Sr. Rose McLarney, CSJ, is the executive director of the Center for Women in Transition at 7529 South Broadway. The center has provided mentoring partnership for women transitioning from the criminal justice system since 1997. The transitional house operated for the women by the center plays a major role in the program's success in keeping participants from getting involved in new crimes. (Photograph by John A. Wright Sr.)

The Grace Hill/Patch Neighborhood Center, at 7925 Minnesota Avenue and established in 1963, takes its name from the old Irish section of Carondelet. The center provides a wide range of services to residents, such as a food pantry, a clothing room, low-cost day care, Head Start, emergency assistance, college courses, a dollar store, and much more. (Photograph by John A. Wright Sr.)

Southern Commercial Bank has been a fixture in Carondelet since 1891. It has provided and continues to provide service, now at two locations in the community. It has been at its present location, at 7201 South Broadway, since 1930. The bank has been instrumental in the publication of two early historical documents written about Carondelet. (Photograph by John A. Wright Sr.)

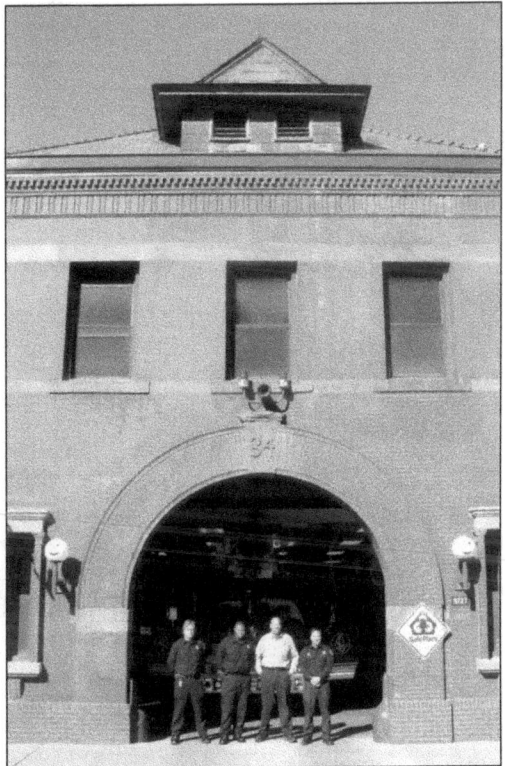

Firehouse No. 34 at 8227 South Broadway is reported to be one of the oldest engine houses in the city of St. Louis. It was dedicated in November 1895. The structure was unchanged until 1969, when a concrete floor was installed to replace the brick pavement. It was completely remodeled and restored in 1988–1989. (Photograph by John A. Wright Sr.)

This market at 7701 South Broadway is the oldest continuously existing marketplace in south St. Louis. It was constructed between 1869 and 1870 as one of the final community projects of the City of Carondelet. It has been somewhat modified in later years with brick extensions on three sides. (Photograph by John A. Wright Sr.)

Quinn Chapel, African Methodist Episcopal, at 225 Bowen Street, which is still used today, was originally built by the City of Carondelet as one of three public marketplaces in 1869. It was purchased by the African Methodist Episcopal Church of Carondelet in 1880 and named to honor the first black Methodist bishop, William Paul Quinn. The belfry was added in 1899. The church was entered on the National Register of Historic Places in 1974. (Photograph by John A. Wright Sr.)

A number of businesses, such as Wicker's Barber Shop at 7718 Ivory Avenue, have called Carondelet home for years. Wicker's Barber Shop may be the oldest continuing barbershop in the city of St. Louis. It was started by Fred Hoelzer in 1889 with the business being continued by his son. In 1961, Charlie Wicker, also known as "Chop-Chop Charlie," pictured here, purchased the building and has been a community fixture ever since. (Photograph by John A. Wright Sr.)

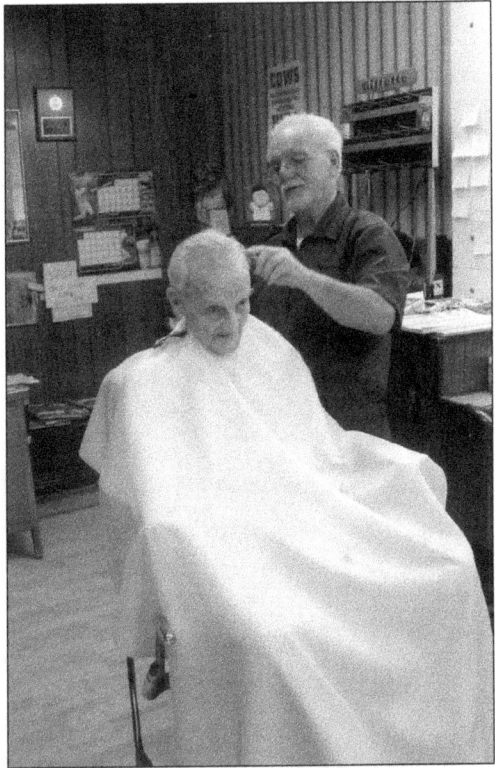

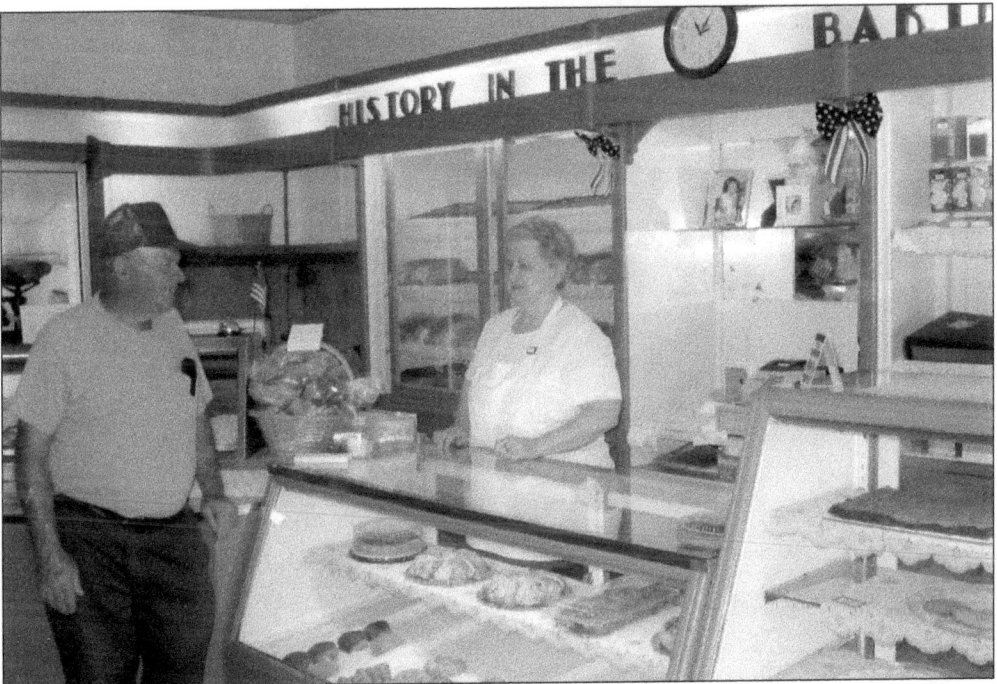

Doering's Bakery, at 7726 Virginia Avenue, has been the home of fine pastry since 1872, when it was established by Jacob Daut. It was owned by several owners before it was purchased in 1945 by Charles Leikam and Herman and Mary Ann Doering. (Photograph by John A. Wright Sr.)

Franz Custom Metal Works, at 6725 South Broadway, is one of the oldest continuous businesses in Carondelet. It was founded by Lorenz Franz about 1887 and continues to be operated by the Franz family today. The elaborate zinc frieze on the cornice of the building was made by the skilled Lorenz Franz. (Photograph by John A. Wright Sr.)

O. W. Rathbone Hardware, at 7625 South Broadway, has been in business since 1904. The store is operated by Vera Heberer and her son Donald. It was started by Vera's grandfather and has been in the family for four generations. In 2006, the store received the 2006 Anchor Business Award in the 11th Ward. (Photograph by John A. Wright Sr.)

Most of the major businesses in Carondelet still remain on South Broadway. This area is gradually making a comeback with a number of investments. (Photograph by John A. Wright Sr.)

Because of the community's location on the river and its access to the railroad, it has many of the desirable attributes major corporations are seeking. (Photograph by John A. Wright Sr.)

The community is fortunate to have a number of schools from which to choose, both public and parochial. Woodward Elementary School, at 725 Bellerive Boulevard, pictured here, serves students from preschool to fifth grade. It was constructed in 1922. (Photograph by John A. Wright Sr.)

Lyons Elementary School, at 7417 Vermont Avenue, is a magnet school in the St. Louis public school system. Lyons was constructed in 1910. It serves students in kindergarten through fifth grade. (Photograph by John A. Wright Sr.)

The Kingshighway United Methodist Church at 900 Bellerive Boulevard has been a part of the Carondelet community for over 125 years, although at different locations and different names. The present property was purchased and a brick chapel was constructed on the site in 1915. Ten years later, the present sanctuary was constructed. (Photograph by John A. Wright Sr.)

St. Cecilia Church at 5418 Louisiana Avenue (pictured here), along with St. Anthony at 3140 Meramec Street and their respective schools, continues to serve the community. The cornerstone for the new St. Cecilia Church was laid in the spring of 1926. The growth of the area was such that the congregation overflowed its old building on Sunday mornings and students the old school. The facility was designed by Henry P. Hess, who designed many buildings for the Archdiocese of St. Louis . (Photograph by John A. Wright Sr.)

The Holly Hills section of the community offers a wide range of homes from the large English-style home pictured to smaller, more modest types. Each year, this section of the community offers a house and garden tour that should not be missed. (Above, photograph by John A. Wright Sr.; left, courtesy of the Carondelet Historical Society)

The historic section of Carondelet offers an enormous selection of homes from the mid-1800s to the present day, ranging from a few rooms to many and from one story to two or three. The choices are unlimited. (Above, courtesy of the Carondelet Historical Society; below, photograph by John A. Wright Sr.)

The Carondelet Historical Center, at 6303 Michigan Avenue, is the home of the Carondelet Historical Society. Since 1981, this former school building has become a museum, archives, and meeting place. This building, constructed in 1873, was once the Des Peres School and the site of the first continuous public school kindergarten in the United States, which was started by Susan Blow. (Photograph by John A. Wright Sr.)

Historical society president and center director Ron Bolte is shown here assisting a visitor engaged in research at the center. The center is a great place to conduct research on Carondelet family roots and area history. (Photograph by John A. Wright Sr.)

The community is going to great lengths to preserve its historical treasures. This structure was moved from the old Monsanto site at Alabama Avenue and Davis Street to the southeast corner of the South St. Louis Square Park in 1992. (Courtesy of the Carondelet Historical Society.)

These homes at 7707–7713 Vulcan Street, which are being preserved, were built in 1850 by mason Henry Zeiss. His family lived in the brick home next door for three generations. The stone quarry firm founded by Zeiss was later bought by the Ruprecht Company. (Photograph by John A. Wright Sr.)

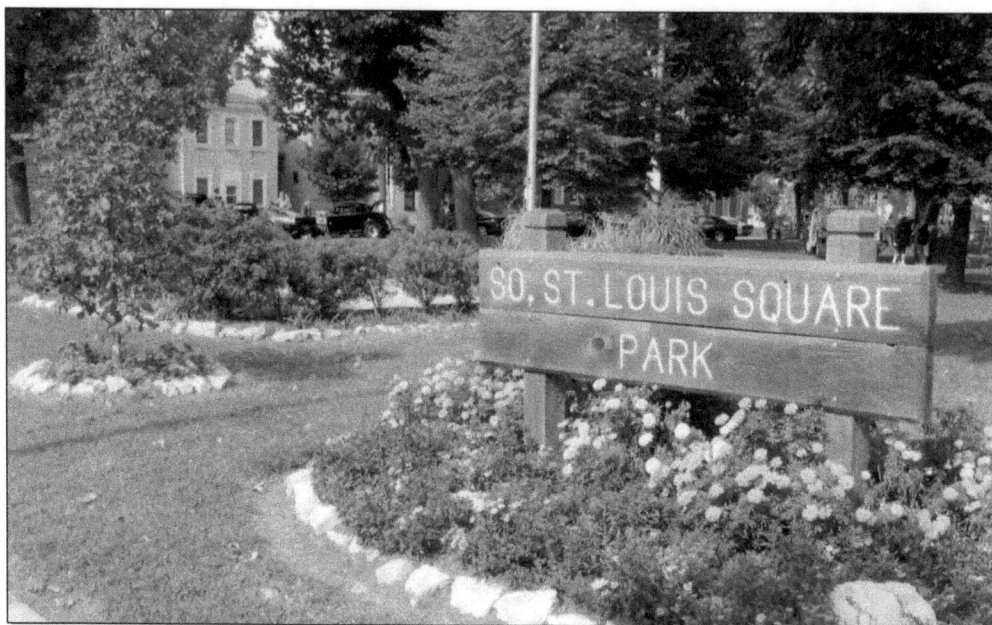

This 1.66-acre square known as South St. Louis Square Park, bounded by South Broadway, Courtois Street, Pennsylvania Avenue, and Schirmer Street, was a gift of the City of Carondelet to St. Louis in 1882. It is part of the original Spanish grant of Carondelet and was forever reserved for park purposes when the town was laid out in 1832. The park today is the site of many community activities. (Photograph by John A. Wright Sr.)

South St. Louis Square Park, pictured here, as well as Carondelet Lions Park, at Davis Street and Michigan Avenue, offers children in the community a place for many hours and days of enjoyment. (Photograph by John A. Wright Sr.)

Carondelet's newest park, Sr. Marie Charles Park at the foot of Elwood Street, provides visitors a lit promenade to enjoy the power and beauty of the Mississippi River firsthand. It is named to honor Sr. Marie Charles, CSJ, past executive director of the Carondelet Community Betterment Federation. For 36 years, she was one of the driving forces behind the organization, which provides an array of activities to highlight and service the community. (Photograph by John A. Wright Sr.)

For a breathtaking view of the river, a trip to Bellerive Park is well worthwhile. This 5.67-acre park was named for St. Agne de Bellerive, a Frenchman who governed the village of St. Louis before the arrival of the first Spanish governor. The park, which was established in 1908, was intended as a starting point for a proposed 1929 riverfront parkway. The plan had to be abandoned because of the Depression. (Photograph by John A. Wright Sr.)

The vest pocket park at the intersection of Ivory Street and Virginia Avenue is the home of St. Louis's last watering trough for horses. The trough has been turned into a fountain and a pleasant focal point for the park. (Photograph by John A. Wright Sr.)

This statue of Albert "Red" Villa, which stands at the western end of the park, pays tribute to the Carondelet leader who spent a major part of his life in devoted service to the community as a businessman and an elected official. (Photograph by John A. Wright Sr.)

The 180-acre Carondelet Park is the third-largest park in the city park system. It offers two large fishing lakes, boat riding, picnic areas, and walking and bike paths, along with a host of other opportunities for outdoor enjoyment. It is also the site of the Alexander Lacy Lyle home, at Grand Boulevard and Loughborough Avenue, which dates back to the 1840s. (Photograph by John A. Wright Sr.)

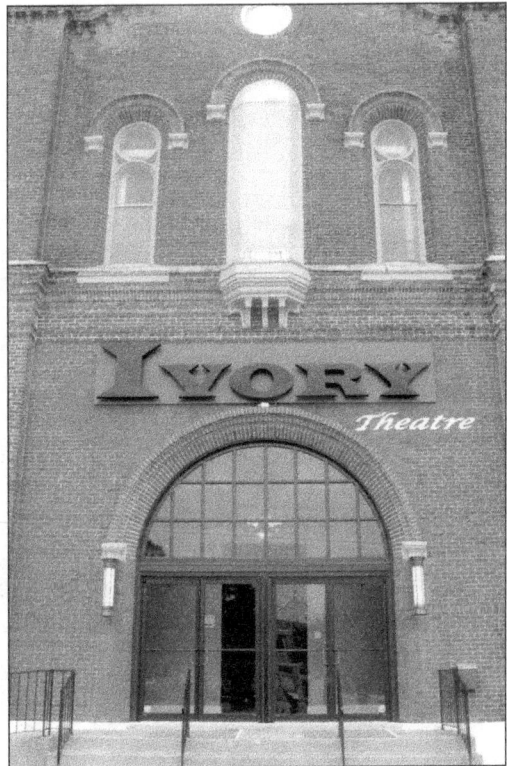

The Ivory Theatre is one of Carondelet's newest renovation projects. The developers invested $800,000 into the project, converting the old St. Boniface Church. They are hoping it will be an anchor for the community with restaurants and bed-and-breakfasts soon following. (Photograph by John A. Wright Sr.)

Alderman Matt Villa is pictured here with his father, state representative Tom Villa, and alderman Fred Wessels (right) of the 13th Ward. Matt Villa is the third generation of his family that has served as an alderman in the 11th Ward and has played an important role in the area's revitalization. (Photograph by John A. Wright Sr.)

In 1991, Sherman George became the city's first black fire chief. George had a distinguished career with the fire department. While the youngest captain in the fire department, he became the city's first black chief instructor at the fire academy since its inception in 1857. As chief instructor, George was in charge of all training programs for the entire fire department and new recruits. George retired from the department in 2007 after 40 years of service. (Courtesy of the City of St. Louis.)

The Carondelet Lions Club, organized on April 23, 1923, and incorporated on August 11, 1926, has been an active organization in the community since its founding. In the last 30 years, the club has purchased approximately $30,000 worth of eyeglasses and given almost $40,000 in food vouchers for Thanksgiving and Christmas. The organization also contributes funds to the Missouri School for the Blind and leader dogs to those in need. Some of its members are pictured here in 2007 picture. (Photograph by John A. Wright Sr.)

Carondelet residents take great pride in their community and make efforts to maintain it. These parents and students are working on the grounds at Blow School during Parents Beautification Day. (Photograph by John A. Wright Sr.)

The Spanish Society is open every day and provides a place for its members to come and fraternize. Members are pictured here enjoying themselves during the society's 80th anniversary celebration. (Photograph by John A. Wright Sr.)

These ladies are members of Las Colaboradoras (the ladies' auxiliary), which was founded in 1937. The original task of the organization was to raise money for the maintenance of the society headquarters and to support the athletic teams. (Courtesy of the Spanish Society.)

The Carondelet Library, at 6800 Michigan Avenue, opened in 1908 with funds from Andrew Carnegie. It contains over 30,000 volumes, art prints, records, and periodicals. Its annual circulation is more than 115,000 per year. The library offers other programs such as preschool story hour, public meeting rooms, and access to the entire public library collection through computers. (Photograph by John A. Wright Sr.)

The annual Fall Auto Show sponsored by the South Broadway Merchants Association at the South St. Louis Square Park on South Broadway is becoming one of the major attractions of the community. It provides an opportunity for visitors to see a lineup of vintage cars. (Photograph by John A. Wright Sr.)

The Carondelet YMCA branch, at 600 Loughborough Avenue, came into existence from the efforts of a community group headed by Theodore Pletcher, Carl Goltermann, Ed Koeln, Thomas Mellow, and James L. Hardie and generous contributions from Mattie E. Johnston and the Liberty Foundry Company. It was constructed in late 1925 and dedicated in 1926. The "Y" offers an array of activities for all ages year-round. (Courtesy of the Carondelet Historical Society.)

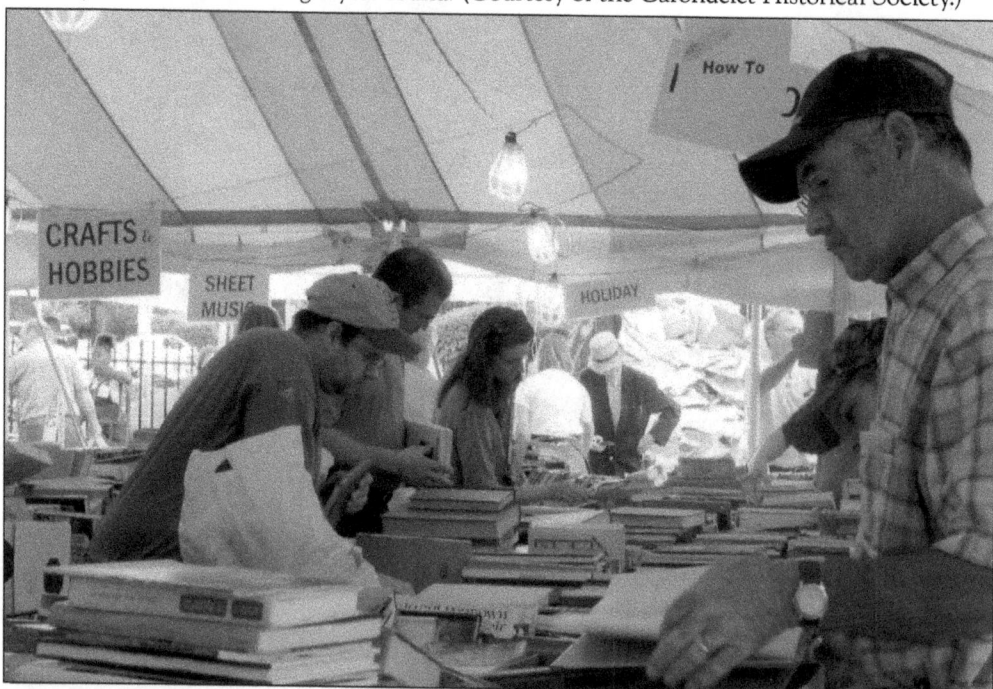

Each year the Carondelet Y sponsors a book fair in the fall to help in the funding of its operations. Each year thousands of fairgoers find books on almost every subject one can imagine among the one million–plus books that are all reasonably priced. (Photograph by John A. Wright Sr.)

Many businessmen, such as Jaymes Dearing, president of the South Broadway Merchants Association, pictured here in front of his renovated office building, have found Carondelet a great place to invest. Dearing has restored a number of properties and placed them on the market. On the left is a picture of his 97-year-old office building before renovation. (Photograph by John A. Wright Sr.)

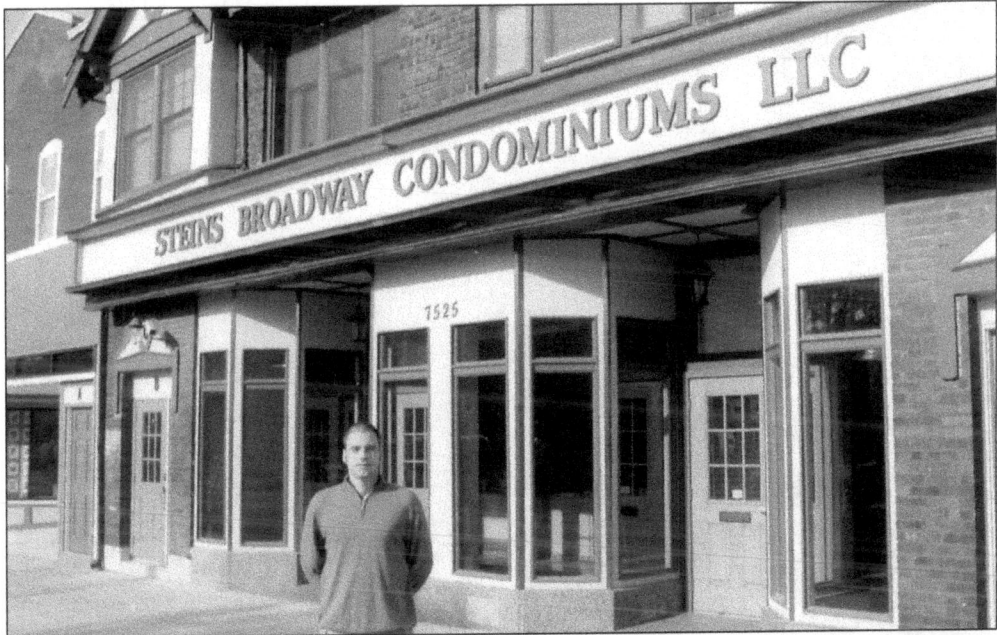

Developer Benjamin Simms, the owner of Steins Broadway Condominiums, LLC, is redeveloping the Steins Broadway Corridor, a three-block mix of more than two dozen residential and commercial buildings at the city's southern end and has rehabbed 50 apartment units in Carondelet. His company plans also to invest $7.5 million in the conversion of the old Carondelet School into luxury apartments. (Photograph by John A. Wright Sr.)

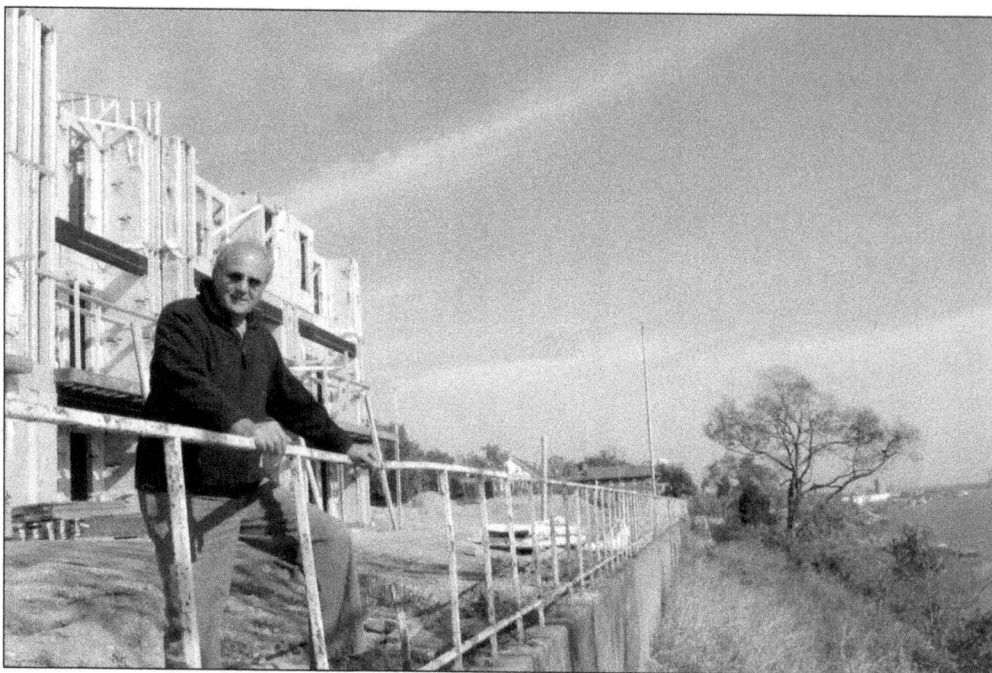

Developer Michael Curran is in the midst of developing 34 town houses, ranging in cost from $450,000 to $600,000, on the river bluffs of South Broadway overlooking the Mississippi River. This $15 million project, a few minutes from downtown, is the first new luxury town house project in the area. Curran is hoping to bring back some of the residential glory of the fine homes that once graced the bluffs. (Photograph by John A. Wright Sr.)

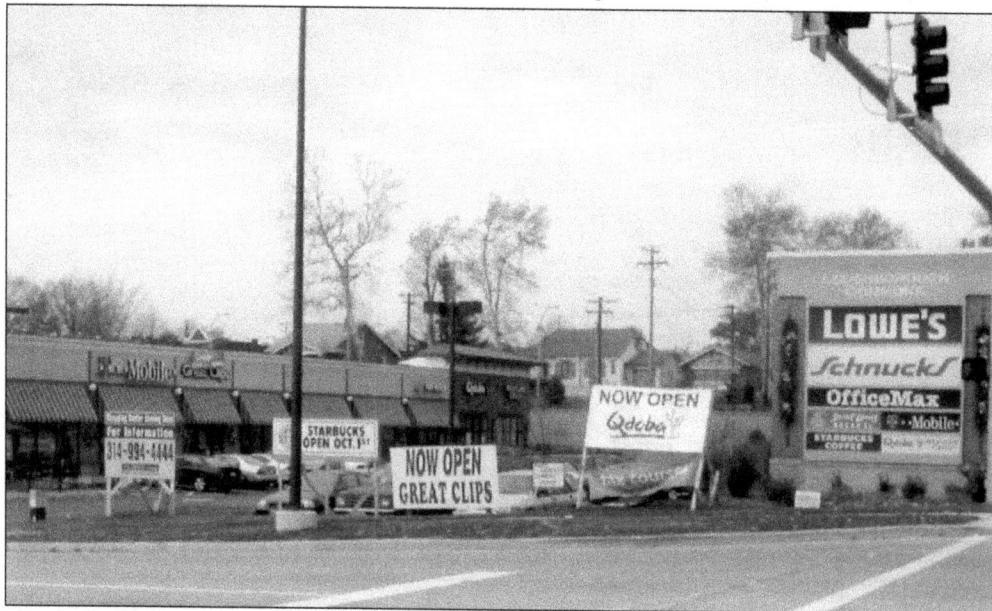

The $40 million Loughborough Commons mall, at Interstate 55 and Loughborough Avenue, anchored by a Schnucks grocery store and a Lowe's hardware store along with a number of smaller stores, is in full operation, bringing an array of services to the community. (Photograph by John A. Wright Sr.)

Carondelet residents look to the future with great optimism, ever mindful of their proud past. Very few communities on this side of the Mississippi River can trace their history back to a time before the Declaration of Independence and to being a part of the United States and living under three flags. (Photograph by John A. Wright Sr.)

The children of Carondelet can take some comfort in knowing that efforts are being made to leave a community for them that they can be proud of and build on for their children and future generations. (Photograph by John A. Wright Sr.)

Visit us at
arcadiapublishing.com

www.ingramcontent.com/pod-product-compliance
Lightning Source LLC
Chambersburg PA
CBHW080607110426
42813CB00006B/1430